TO:

FROM:

DATE:

Published by Christian Art Publishers
PO Box 1599, Vereeniging, 1930, RSA

© 2018
First edition 2018

Designed by Christian Art Publishers

Images used under license from Shutterstock.com

Unless otherwise indicated, Scripture quotations are taken from
the *Holy Bible*, English Standard Version. Copyright © 2001
by Crossway Bibles, a publishing ministry of Good News Publishers.
Used by permission. All rights reserved.

Scripture quotations marked NIV are taken from the *Holy Bible*,
New International Version® NIV®. Copyright © 1973, 1978, 1984, 2011
by International Bible Society. Used by permission of Biblica, Inc.®
All rights reserved worldwide.

Printed in China

ISBN 978-1-4321-2838-8

18 19 20 21 22 23 24 25 26 27 – 10 9 8 7 6 5 4 3 2 1

KNOWING

Jesus

FINDING FRIENDSHIP WITH THE SON OF GOD

Nancy Taylor
& Philip Ryken

**CHRISTIAN ART
PUBLISHERS**

CONTENTS

Questions about What Jesus Did and Taught

Questions about What Difference Jesus Makes to Me

INTRODUCTION

This book was my sister Nancy's idea. As a mother of five, she hears lots of questions every day. In my role as the President of Wheaton College, I hear lots of questions too, including theological questions.

The most important questions that anyone can ask are about Jesus: *Who is Jesus? How do we know He really existed? Why do people call Him "Christ"? Was He really the Son of God? Why did He die on the cross, and did He really rise from the dead? Where is Jesus now? Will we ever see Him again?*

The answers to these questions help us understand the meaning of our existence and open the door to eternal life. But they are only the beginning. Once we enter into a personal friendship with Jesus, we want to learn as much about Him as we can, and one of the best ways to learn is by asking more questions: *Why did Jesus come to earth as a baby? Could Jesus sin? What did He look like? How could He be both human and divine? If He is truly God, then why did He need to pray?* And so on.

We hope that this book will help give some answers. We wrote it mainly for people who are new to Christianity, but it is really for anyone who is curious about Jesus and wants to know Him better.

There are sixty questions in all – just the right number for reading one question (and one answer) every day for two months. We have tried to put plenty of Scripture into our answers – partly because the Bible is the only place to get reliable information about Jesus, and partly because we hope that some people will use this book for their daily devotions.

Nancy did most of the writing, and I did most of the editing. So I suppose our relationship is typical: the younger sibling does most of the work, while the older sibling makes the corrections and takes half the credit.

But we wrote this book for you. And our prayer for you is simply this: that you will come to know Jesus in a deeper way, and that you will never stop wanting to know Him better and better.

~ Philip Ryken

QUESTIONS

ABOUT WHO

Jesus

IS

1

Who is Jesus?

We're starting off with the big question that this whole book seeks to answer, and in fact the question that is central to your entire life. Maybe you picked up this book hoping to settle in your own mind and heart the answer to this question, and getting the answer right is the most important thing you will do in your whole life: Who is Jesus?

The question is not who *was* Jesus, as if He were just a historical character, but who *is* Jesus? And how do His life and death make a difference today and for the rest of forever? John sums up the purpose of his Gospel – and we could say the whole Bible – with these words: "these are written so that you may believe that Jesus is the Christ, the Son of God, and that by believing you may have life in his name" (Jn. 20:31).

In this verse we learn that Jesus is God, the eternally existent, all-powerful Creator of all things. The New Testament writers took this fact for granted. Jesus is also man, born at a particular time and place in history, as proven by historical evidence. He lived and ministered in the first century A.D., died on a cross, was buried, and rose again three days later. After He appeared to people on earth He ascended into heaven. Jesus is God in the flesh who came to live with us on earth and die for our sins on the cross.

But for us, perhaps the most important answer to the question "who is Jesus?" comes in the last phrase of John 20:31: "by believing you may have life in his name." Jesus is God's solution to fixing the relationship that our sin fatally ruined. We were created to live in perfect, harmonious union with God, but our sin made that type of connection with a holy God impossible. But then Jesus bridged the gap, paying the price for our sin and making it once again possible for us to have a relationship with God.

If you confess with your mouth that Jesus is Lord and believe in your heart that God raised him from the dead, you will be saved.
ROMANS 10:9

Christians are not people who adhere to a set of rules, but rather people who know Jesus, who believe that He is the God who entered history to make it possible for sinners like us to know Him and become acceptable to a holy God, and who lives eternally as our Lord.

When we accept Jesus as our Lord and Savior, we receive the ability to live free from sin and know that we are fully and deeply loved by God. Jesus is the one who gives us life.

2

How do we know Jesus really existed?

If the Christian life is a love relationship with Jesus, then we want to know the facts about Him as well as to believe by faith that He is who He says He is. A good place to start is to learn what we can know about His life in Palestine in the first century A.D.

Textual and archaeological evidence repeatedly affirms the historical reliability of the New Testament's account of Jesus' life and work. The Roman senator and historian Tacitus refers to Christ, to His execution at the hands of Pontius Pilate, and to the presence of Christians in Rome, in his famous Annals. The Jewish-Roman historian Josephus includes references to Jesus and John the Baptist in his *Antiquities of the Jews*.

Another way to go about proving the historical reliability of the Biblical accounts of Jesus is to consider the eyewitness accounts given in the Gospels. If a person wanted to create a book that would prove a person's existence, they might offer unwaveringly supportive witnesses.

Instead, the Gospels repeatedly show men who doubted Jesus' deity and had to be convinced of it. The disciples in His inner circle were hardly the kind of people a leader would choose to lead a revolution – fishermen, hated tax collectors, and even women (who in those days were treated as second-class citizens). But then these same former doubters were willing to die rather than to recant their faith in a man with whom they had lived and ministered for three years. No one who lived that closely with a fraud would be willing to die for something they knew was a lie. Then there is the content of the Gospels themselves. These books, written at different times and from vastly different perspectives, offer a cohesive picture of a man who claimed to be the one true God.

Furthermore, the most space is given to His legal condemnation and shameful death – surely not the parts of a story that someone would highlight if they were trying to aggrandize the life of a mere teacher.

When taken all together, the historical reliability of Jesus' life leads us to one conclusion: He was God in human form, who was born and lived and died to reveal God to us.

Faith in Jesus is logical and reasonable. This gives His followers a quiet confidence to face hardship and struggle with peace and joy.

For I delivered to you as of first importance what I also received: that Christ died for our sins in accordance with the Scriptures, that he was buried, that he was raised on the third day in accordance with the Scriptures, and that he appeared to Cephas, then to the twelve.

1 CORINTHIANS 15:3-5

3

What does it mean that Jesus was the firstborn over creation?

In the ancient Near East, as in some cultures today, the oldest son held a position of honor in a family. Upon his father's death, the firstborn would inherit his father's authority and responsibilities. He would also inherit a double portion of the family estate. If his father happened to be a king, the firstborn son inherited his throne and became the new ruler over the kingdom.

According to Jewish law the firstborn was dedicated to God in remembrance for the way God passed over the homes of the Israelites and spared their sons when He struck down the firstborn of the Egyptians. God declared, "all the firstborn are mine. On the day that I struck down all the firstborn in the land of Egypt, I consecrated for my own all the firstborn in Israel, both of man and of beast. They shall be mine: I am the LORD" (Num. 3:13). In this way, the firstborn was a representative of his brothers and sisters, like a tithe given back to the Lord.

Jesus was physically the firstborn son of Mary (Lk. 2:7), which is how He was able to be born of a virgin. But more importantly He was the firstborn of Creation (Col. 1:15). This term does not signify that God the Son was born into existence, for Jesus is the eternally existent God, the preexistent Creator. Rather, it indicates His priority. Jesus is the ruler over all things because He is the Creator of all things. The next verse reads, "For by him all things were created, in heaven and on earth, visible and invisible, whether thrones or dominions or rulers or authorities – all things were created through him and for him" (Col. 1:16).

The term "firstborn" also signifies that Jesus retains all the rights of an oldest son in the culture of His day. He receives honor from God the Father and shares in His glory (Phil. 2:9; Rev. 5:12). He sits on the throne of His Father and rules over heaven and earth (Ps. 110:1; Rev. 3:21). He has inherited "all things" (Heb. 1:1-4). Finally, as the firstborn Son Jesus became our representative offering to God, dying in our place so that we might be spared (1 Pet. 2:24).

For those whom he foreknew he also predestined to be conformed to the image of his Son, in order that he might be the firstborn among many brothers.

ROMANS 8:29

Remarkably, Jesus shares this glorious inheritance with us. He died not only to save us, but also to make us God's adopted children who will share His full inheritance. Paul wrote to the Romans, "we are children of God, and if children, then heirs – heirs of God and fellow heirs with Christ" (Rom. 8:16-17). Jesus did not keep all the glory for Himself, He shares it all with us (2 Cor. 3:18; 2 Thess. 2:14; Heb. 2:10). We live in the expectation of a vast inheritance – a rich promise that calls us to gratitude and generosity.

4

Where is Jesus mentioned in the Old Testament?

One of the things that makes the Bible the most amazing book ever written is that even though it was written by many different people over hundreds of years, it presents a cohesive picture of the condition of human beings (utterly sinful and in need of salvation) and of the character and work of God (perfectly just and at the same time showing mercy).

Throughout the Old Testament we learn more and more about God's plan to save us, centered on the Messiah or "Anointed One." The story of salvation is like a puzzle gradually taking shape, with God putting in one piece at a time until the whole picture comes together in the New Testament. Once you know what to look for, every page of the Bible helps you see Jesus.

God first promised a Savior in the Garden of Eden, immediately after sin entered the world (Gen. 3:15). There, God promised to send a deliverer to crush Satan. Then He revealed that this Messiah would come through the family of Abraham (Gen. 12:3) and later through Isaac (Gen. 17:19), Jacob (Num. 24:17), and King David (2 Sam. 7:12-13). In addition to His ancestral line, the Messiah was promised to be born of a virgin (Isa. 7:14) in Bethlehem (Mic. 5:2), to spend time in Egypt (Hos. 11:1), and to suffer and die (Ps. 22; Isa. 53).

For to us a child is born, to us a son is given; and the government shall be upon his shoulder, and his name shall be called Wonderful Counselor, Mighty God, Everlasting Father, Prince of Peace.

ISAIAH 9:6

After three days He would rise again (Ps. 16:10; 49:15). In all, scholars have identified more than 300 specific Old Testament prophecies about the Messiah that Jesus fulfilled. It's almost like a fingerprint: the odds against one person fulfilling even a few of these prophecies made hundreds of years before His birth – let alone all of them – are astronomical. It just couldn't happen ... except that it did, and Jesus was the man. No one else before or in the future could possibly fulfill all of the Old Testament prophecies that Jesus fulfilled because of the specific time and place in which He lived and died and rose again.

The prophecies about Jesus confirm that the Christian faith is reasonable and reliable. You don't have to check your brain at the door in order to become a Christian. In fact, the more you study the Bible, the more you realize that it takes more faith *not* to believe in Jesus than to believe Him!

5

What do the genealogies in Matthew and Luke tell us about Jesus?

People like to know where they came from. We trace family genealogies to discover our ancestry and to see if there are any surprises in our ethnicity. We go to family reunions and recount old stories. We are looking for a sense of belonging and rootedness, and perhaps for reminders of God's faithfulness throughout the generations.

As important as genealogies are to us, they were even more important to the Jews in Jesus' day. Lists of ancestors told who people were – their identity. More than just serving as a record of which tribe they belonged to, genealogies assured them that they were part of God's people – descended through Abraham, Isaac, and Jacob – and thus heirs of the promises of God.

The Bible gives us two genealogies for Jesus, one in Matthew and one in Luke. These genealogies differ significantly, which has led some people to doubt their veracity. There are two possible ways to reconcile these discrepancies: 1) Matthew gives the legal descendants of David, the heirs to David's throne who were not necessarily related, while Luke gives the biological bloodline. According to this theory, Matthew is proving that Jesus is the rightful heir of David's throne, while Luke is simply listing each person's father. 2) Alternatively, Luke is recording Mary's family tree, since Jesus was the son of Mary and the Son of God rather than the son of Joseph. Meanwhile, Matthew's genealogy traces the line through Joseph. In this case, Mary and Joseph were distant cousins, both descendants of David, and thus Jesus had a double claim to the throne – both by legal succession and by blood.

Jesus, when he began his ministry, was about thirty years of age, being the son (as was supposed) of Joseph, the son of Heli.

LUKE 3:23

Readers sometimes question the inclusion of genealogies in the Gospels. We are tempted to skip over them as we read, glossing over the hard-to-pronounce names so we can get to the more exciting parts of the Gospels. However, the genealogies of Jesus serve important purposes. They show our Savior's humanity. Jesus was a real, flesh-and-blood human being who walked the earth at a particular time in history. He was one of us.

But Jesus was not merely a man. Luke's genealogy ends with these words: "the son of Adam, the Son of God" (Lk. 3:38). Jesus was both God and man, the new Adam who came to save broken humanity. Jesus had to become one of us to save us, facing the same temptations we do, yet not succumbing to them so He could be the perfect sacrifice and bear the total punishment for our sin. The genealogies show that Jesus is able to save anyone who trusts in Him: the only God-man, who became the perfect sacrifice for sin.

6

Why is the virgin birth important?

The Biblical account teaches that Mary became pregnant with Jesus supernaturally, through an act of the Holy Spirit, while she was still a virgin. It does not teach that she always remained a virgin, only that she was a virgin until the birth of Christ (Mt. 1:18, 20, 25). Her virginity fulfilled the prophecy of Isaiah that said, "Therefore the Lord himself will give you a sign. Behold, the virgin shall conceive and bear a son, and shall call his name Immanuel" (Isa. 7:14). In Isaiah's prophecy the virgin birth is a clear sign that this child is the Son of God – God with us.

People today try to discount anything miraculous or supernatural, questioning the Biblical account and saying that such things could not happen. But they miss the point. The very unlikeliness of a miracle is what proves that it is an act of God. Others argue that since only two Gospels mention the virgin birth it must not have happened, while ignoring the fact that the virgin birth is nowhere discounted or argued against in Scripture.

If we are going to believe the Bible we have to believe all of it, both the believable and the miraculous. The virgin birth happens to be a particularly important event in the Gospel account.

Carl F. H. Henry, a prominent evangelical theologian, argues that the virgin birth is the "essential, historical indication of the Incarnation, bearing not only an analogy to the divine and human natures of the Incarnate, but also bringing out the nature, purpose, and bearing of this work of God to salvation."

Why is the doctrine of the virgin birth so essential to our faith? First, it is a declaration that this person – Jesus Christ – is a supernatural being. Even His beginning is miracu-

And the angel answered her, "The Holy Spirit will come upon you, and the power of the Most High will overshadow you; therefore the child to be born will be called holy – the Son of God."

LUKE 1:35

lous, and there are many more miracles to come. In addition, it is a sign of God's redemption. We need a Savior, but the human race cannot produce one itself; we need God to provide one for us.

Finally, the virgin birth signifies a new beginning. Jesus is not a continuation of what has gone before, but a divine intervention. Here is something new: God taking on human flesh to save us. Here is a man born of a woman like other humans, but also born of God the Holy Spirit, unlike anyone else who ever lived. Here is someone with the necessary credentials to be a Savior.

7

Why did Jesus come to earth as a baby?

Try to imagine the angels' reaction to the birth of Jesus Christ in a Bethlehem stable. Don't you suspect that they expected God's plan to be more glorious? Surely it was enough for the Son of God to lower Himself to the level of an earthly king. Didn't He at least deserve a little pomp and circumstance? Couldn't He have avoided the indignity of being born as a helpless baby, and an impoverished one at that?

But God's plan was better. John 1:14 says, "the Word became flesh and dwelt among us" – literally, He "pitched His tent" among us. The eternal God emptied Himself to be born in the likeness of a man and to live with us (Phil. 2:5-7). Jesus was born as a baby so that He could experience all of human life – the messy parts as well as the good parts, the growing and maturing as well as the adulthood. When we really think about it, we realize that the sacrifice Jesus made on our behalf wasn't only the cross; it was also living among us and becoming one of us.

Jesus' birth as a baby accomplished two things. First, in order to save us He had to become one of us. The only sacrifice that could pay the penalty our sins deserve was the life of a perfect human being. The law demanded that someone with genuine humanity needed to face every difficulty and temptation of human existence and remain sinless. That perfection, offered as a sacrifice to God, could pay the penalty for every sinner and reverse the curse of the Fall. By growing up from a baby to an adult, Jesus fully demonstrated His humanity and authentically entered into humanity so He could save us.

Second, the "growing up" of Jesus enabled Him to sympathize fully with everything we face in life. Hebrews 4:15 says, "For we do not have a high priest who is unable to sympathize with our weaknesses, but one who in every respect has been tempted as we are, yet without sin." This is one of the ways God "remembers that we are dust" (Ps. 103:14). Every trial we encounter, every temptation we face, every pain we suffer, Jesus truly understands. He lived through it all Himself.

And she gave birth to her firstborn son and wrapped him in swaddling cloths and laid him in a manger, because there was no place for them in the inn.

LUKE 2:7

He was poor; He was an outcast. He was tempted and tried. He witnessed brutality and hopelessness. He was tired and stressed and needed rest. He even tasted death. When we feel discouraged and wonder where God is in the midst of our pain, we can look to Jesus and remember that He loved us so much He was willing to go through it all with us and for us. What great love Jesus showed in sacrificing Himself to such an extreme degree!

8

How could Jesus be both God and man?

The Gospel accounts of the birth of Jesus Christ emphasize the fact that He is "God with us" (Mt. 1:23). Jesus is not an abstract idea or force. He is not a myth. He is not God disguised as a human. He is not part God and part man. Jesus Christ has two complete natures – human and divine – in one person. This mysterious union of two natures (the theological term for this is "hypostatic union," which literally means *personal union*) is possible because He was conceived by the Holy Spirit and born of a virgin.

The phrase "conceived by the Holy Spirit" means that Jesus had no earthly father. He did have a heavenly Father – God the Father – with whom He was eternally coexistent. He was not created by God – in fact, Jesus created all things with the Father and the Spirit. Nor was Jesus born from God; He *is* God. And somehow, through the miraculous work of the Holy Spirit, He entered Mary's womb. He became a baby. God spoke, and the Word became flesh. This mystery demonstrates Jesus' deity because only the holy Son of God could be conceived in this way.

The virgin birth shows us that Jesus was also human. He gestated and grew like any other baby. He was born one night in Bethlehem, in the humblest circumstances, to a young and inexperienced mother. He grew and learned just like any other Jewish boy of that time (Lk. 2:52). He suffered and struggled and was tempted, just as we are (Heb. 4:15). He had painful and jubilant emotions (Lk. 10:21; Jn. 11:33-35).

And the Word became flesh and dwelt among us, and we have seen his glory, glory as of the only Son from the Father, full of grace and truth.

JOHN 1:14

He grew tired and hungry (Jn. 4:6; Mt. 4:2). Jesus took on all the limitations of human flesh, including the pains of death. But there is of course one key difference between Jesus and us: He was sinless (Heb. 4:15).

In the end, it is a mystery how Jesus could be both God and man. We can't fully understand how these two natures coexist in one person. In this, as in so many other ways, our finite minds cannot comprehend the ways of God. But we can believe this mystery by faith because it is what the Bible teaches. God the Son, the divine Creator, took on flesh and became a human at a particular point in history, living among His creatures.

Why would the all-powerful God give up heaven to live on this fallen earth with all the limitations of finite human existence? The Immortal contained in mortal flesh. Almighty God and helpless babe. It is unthinkable and incomprehensible. Yet it shows how intensely God wanted to be in a relationship with us. He took on humanity to save humanity. He became fully a man so He could fully save us. He became God with us so that one day we can be with Him. This is the glorious mystery of the incarnation.

9

Did Jesus have any brothers or sisters?

We often think of Jesus ministering among the throngs of people, or in a small group with His disciples. But Jesus had a family, too. The New Testament lists James, Joses, Simon, and Judas as his brothers, and also mentions "sisters" who are not named (Mk. 6:3). These would have been Jesus' "half-siblings," the children of His mother Mary and His earthly stepfather Joseph.

When the book of Hebrews tells us that Jesus was tempted in every way just as we are, this includes the very real temptation for retaliation or revenge brought on by irritating younger siblings (Heb. 4:15). Jesus' humanity included the joys and trials of living in a large family.

At first, Jesus' siblings were skeptical of His divinity. They wondered if He was out of His mind (Mk. 3:21) and dishonored His ministry (Mt. 13:54-58). But after the resurrection, they were convinced that He was the Son of God. They expressed this newfound faith by devoting themselves to prayer (Acts 1:14). Siblings of Jesus are later mentioned as ministers in the church (Gal. 1:19; 1 Cor. 9:5). Most notable is the writer of the epistle of

James, who is generally thought to be the half-brother of Jesus mentioned in Mark 6:3 and Matthew 13:55. The author of the epistle of Jude identifies himself as the brother of James, so most scholars conclude that he is the Judas mentioned in those same passages. Both James and Jude call themselves not only brothers, but also servants of Christ (James 1:1; Jude 1). Clearly, these physical half-brothers had become convinced that Jesus was who He said He was, for they devoted their lives to telling others about Him.

Remarkably, all true Christians are also brothers and sisters of Jesus. When we accept Jesus as our Savior, we are adopted into God's family. His Father becomes our Father. At the moment of salvation we receive a change in status: we are no longer slaves of sin and enemies of God, but are instantly adopted into God's family. We become His children: "So you are no longer a slave, but a son, and if a son, then an heir through God" (Gal. 4:7). As His children, we have all the rights and privileges that a beloved son would have enjoyed in Jesus' day. We are suddenly free to call God our Father (Rom. 8:15; Gal. 4:6).

> *The Spirit himself bears witness with our spirit that we are children of God, and if children, then heirs – heirs of God and fellow heirs with Christ, provided we suffer with him in order that we may also be glorified with him.*
>
> ROMANS 8:16-17

We share the inheritance of eternal life (Tit. 3:7), which includes all the promises of God (Heb. 6:17) and blessings of His kingdom (James 2:5). Jesus died so that we could share in His inheritance, receiving the full rights of sons. What a gift it is to be called children of God! As the brothers and sisters of Jesus, we are sons and daughters of the Most High God, and therefore the princes and princesses of His royal kingdom.

10

What was Jesus' childhood like?

Hebrews 2:17 tells us that Jesus "had to be made like his brothers in every respect, so that he might become a merciful and faithful high priest in the service of God, to make propitiation for the sins of the people." In other words, Jesus did not merely resemble human beings; He really was a human being! He was born as a baby, grew up as a boy, and became a man. This progression has significant implications for His childhood.

Jesus grew up like any other boy (Lk. 2:52). As an infant He depended on His parents for everything and had to be taught how to eat, walk, and talk – just like any other baby. His body, mind, and emotions had to mature just like anyone else's. He grew up in a family with brothers and sisters who sometimes didn't get along, and with parents who were imperfect and sometimes grew impatient with Him. His childhood was filled with the same things as any other Jewish boy in His day. He was circumcised when He was eight days old (Lk. 2:21).

His family celebrated Jewish religious holidays with their extended family. Every year His family made a pilgrimage to Jerusalem for the Feast of the Passover (Lk. 2:41). The boy Jesus was taught the Jewish Scriptures, as well as how to read and write.

Joseph, the earthly stepfather of Jesus, was a carpenter, so it is likely that Jesus learned that trade (Mt. 13:55; Mk. 6:3). Carpenters would have been responsible for building the wooden frameworks on which stones were placed to erect buildings, as well as wooden tables, stools, carts, or other necessities.

The small sacrifice given at Jesus' circumcision shows that His family was too poor to bring a more extravagant offering (Lev. 12:8; Lk. 2:24). Jesus grew up in a small town as the son of a tradesman, giving Him the ability to understand the daily life and financial struggles of a humble family.

Jesus experienced all the joys and trials of growing up as a human being, and because of this He is able to sympathize fully with everything that we go through. He faced every temptation that we face – a perspective that enables Him to show great mercy toward us. But of course Jesus wasn't just a boy who grew up to be a man. He was also God – and as a result He lived a holy life. Because of His sinless perfection, He was able to "make propitiation for the sins of the people" – in other words, to fulfill the holy law's demands and then take our sin on Himself and bear the wrath of God in our place.

Jesus secured our salvation by subjecting Himself to the limitations of human flesh while retaining all the holiness of God.

And the child grew and became strong, filled with wisdom. And the favor of God was upon him.

LUKE 2:40

11

Was Jesus married?

Dan Brown's best-selling novel *The DaVinci Code* (2003) raised the question of whether Jesus could have been married to Mary Magdalene. Then, in 2012, Harvard Divinity School historian Karen L. King unveiled a manuscript fragment that supposedly read "Jesus said to them, 'My wife …'" Scholars subsequently tested the manuscript (dubbed the *Gospel of Jesus' Wife*) and determined it to be a forgery, but the rumors continue. Could Jesus have been married?

Most theologians agree that Jesus was not married. Surely the Gospels would have mentioned such an important fact, if only in passing. Yet there is no mention of a wife. Nor is there any hint of a special relationship between Jesus and Mary Magdalene, as some have alleged.

Furthermore, Jesus is portrayed as a traveling teacher – hardly the lifestyle a respectable Jewish husband would have led in those days. Jesus was essentially homeless, and since the Biblical mandate is for husbands to provide for their wives (Gen. 3:17; Eph. 5:25), we can reasonably infer that His lifestyle would have looked far different if He had been married. A wife would have interfered with His mission to lay down His life for His friends, so it was God's will for Jesus to be single.

There is a lesson for us in our Savior's marital status. Jesus lived a full and meaningful life, fulfilling God's will in every way, as a single person. He enjoyed close familial relationships with His friends in the community of believers. He said, "Here are my mother and my brothers! For whoever does the will of my Father in heaven is my brother and sister and mother" (Mt. 12:49-50).

There were women as well as men in His intimate circle of friends. They ate and drank, lived and worked together. Marriage and family life is a noble and even Biblical goal, but it isn't for everyone. Jesus' life shows us that God's will for some people is singleness, and this too is a good gift from Him.

Perhaps the main reason why Jesus never married on earth is because His bride is the church. Paul used this imagery – which was frequently used in the Old Testament to describe God's love for His people – specifically of Christ in Ephesians 5:25-27: "Husbands, love your wives, as Christ loved the church and gave himself up for her, that he might sanctify her, having cleansed her by the washing of water with the word, so that he might present the church to himself in splendor, without spot or wrinkle or any such thing, that she might be holy and without blemish."

"Let us rejoice and exult and give him the glory, for the marriage of the Lamb has come, and his Bride has made herself ready; it was granted her to clothe herself with fine linen, bright and pure" – for the fine linen is the righteous deeds of the saints. And the angel said to me, "Write this: Blessed are those who are invited to the marriage supper of the Lamb." And he said to me, "These are the true words of God."

REVELATION 19:7-9

Jesus' earthly singleness serves to show how much He loved us. He died to save the one true bride that He faithfully loves: the church. He gave Himself for us and now He invites us to give ourselves to Him.

12

What do we know about Jesus' physical appearance?

If you grew up going to church, you probably have in your mind a picture of Jesus that matches whatever artist's depiction of Him that used to hang on your Sunday school room wall. Chances are good that He was portrayed as a member of your church's majority ethnic group. Did you ever wonder how closely that picture matched the depiction we have of Jesus from the Bible?

We do not and cannot really know what Jesus looked like. The Bible doesn't specifically say. And that's probably a good thing. If we had a detailed description of His physical appearance we would probably fight over which artist's rendering was more true to the description in Scripture. The mystery surrounding Jesus' appearance also helps us look forward to seeing Him face-to-face in Heaven. One thing we can know is that if Jesus' appearance were important to our understanding of Him – and if it were better for us to have a physical description of Him – the Gospels would have given us one.

Isaiah 53:2 says, "He had no form or majesty that we should look at him, and no beauty that we should desire him." This may be mainly a reference to what Jesus looked like at the crucifixion, when His body was disfigured by abuse and pain, but it does tell us that the beauty of Jesus' physical appearance isn't what draws us to Him. We are drawn to His character, His holiness, His love.

We know from the account of Jesus in the Garden of Gethsemane that He was hard to tell apart from His disciples (Mt. 26:48-49). He looked like other Galilean Semites who lived in the first century. Scientists have recently come up with a composite of what men looked like in that region in Jesus' day. They think He was probably about 5'1" (1.5m) tall, with dark eyes and dark skin. Given the style of the day, He most likely had a beard and short hair (see 1 Cor. 11:14).

[Jesus] had no form or majesty that we should look at him, and no beauty that we should desire him. He was despised and rejected by men; a man of sorrows, and acquainted with grief; and as one from whom men hide their faces he was despised, and we esteemed him not.

ISAIAH 53:2-3

The most important thing to know about what Jesus looked like is that He was not made in our image. Rather, we are made in His image. Romans 8:29 says, "For those whom he foreknew he also predestined to be conformed to the image of his Son, in order that he might be the firstborn among many brothers." We may have an attractive image that we would like Him to resemble. But instead of trying to make Jesus fit into our mold of beauty, we should be striving to look more like Him. He is the standard, not us.

First John 3:2 reminds us that one day we really will look like Jesus: "we know that when he appears we shall be like him, because we shall see him as he is." The more we look at His character and majesty, the more closely we will resemble Him.

13

Did Jesus always know that He was God?

John opens his gospel with a clear declaration of Jesus' deity – His identity as God the Son: "In the beginning was the Word, and the Word was with God, and the Word was God" (1:1). Jesus was the eternal God even before He took on human flesh. From the perspective of His eternal pre-existence, the Son of God always knew that He was very God of very God. But what about His earthly existence? The question of when during His earthly life Jesus knew that He was the Son of God is not specifically addressed in Scripture. Perhaps we can infer the answer.

When Jesus took on human flesh, He subjected Himself to certain limitations on His knowledge. Luke 2:52 says that Jesus grew in wisdom – something that would have been impossible if He had not put aside some of His omniscience to become human. As part of His human experience, Jesus voluntarily put Himself in a position of needing to learn like other children and adolescents. He submitted Himself to knowing only what the Father revealed to Him by the Holy Spirit. In this way, and in many others, Jesus became like us and experienced human learning and limited understanding.

Yet even from His youth, Jesus seemed to have a clear sense of His nature and work. When He went to the Temple and talked with the teachers, "all who heard him were amazed at his understanding and his answers" (Lk. 2:47). Even as an adolescent, Jesus taught with great wisdom and depth of understanding. Furthermore, He told His worried parents that He needed to be "in my Father's house" (v. 49). No one in His day would have called Almighty God "my Father"! But Jesus did, because He was already aware of His special, intimate relationship with God the Father. We can conclude from the story of Jesus in the Temple that He came to an early understanding of His true identity as the Son of God.

Perhaps some of Jesus' early understanding of His identity came from the witness of others. Angels sang at His birth (Lk. 2:8-15), Anna and Simeon called Him a king (Lk. 2:22-38), and the Magi gave Him kingly gifts (Mt. 2). Surely Mary told Jesus about these events from an early age. Later came the witness of John the Baptist (Jn. 1:29-34) and the Holy Spirit (Lk. 3:22), who both testified to His deity.

And Jesus increased in wisdom and in stature and in favor with God and man.

LUKE 2:52

Regardless of the exact moment of Jesus' self-knowledge of His identity as the Son of God, it is clear that He did know Himself to be God by the time He was an adult. This explains why He called Himself "I AM" (Jn. 8:58) and spoke of being with God the Father in glory before creation (Jn. 17:5). Based on the witness of Jesus Himself, the Holy Spirit, and other eyewitnesses, we can know that Jesus is indeed God the Son, who is worthy and able to take away our sins and reconcile us to God.

14

Could Jesus sin?

The Bible tells us that Jesus did not sin, and that is why He was able to perfectly atone for our sin. But sometimes theologians like to consider and debate questions like, "Was it possible for Jesus to have sinned? If He was truly a human being, was it possible for Him to have sinned and thus to have been unable to become the fit sacrifice for our sins?"

There are different ways of looking at this question. One is to consider whether Jesus was mentally and physically capable of sinning. Scholars agree on the answer to this question: yes, because He was human. But if we ask, "Was Jesus morally capable of sinning?" that answer is less straightforward.

We know that Jesus was tempted. Matthew 4 outlines the temptation of Jesus at the hands of Satan just before He began His public ministry. Hebrews 4:15 says further that Jesus "in every respect has been tempted as we are, yet without sin." James assures us that temptation is not sin (1:13-15). Therefore, it is not a moral problem that Jesus was tempted. In fact, it is a good thing from our perspective, because it means that He understands our temptations and can show us how to withstand temptation (see Mt. 4).

Most theologians believe that Jesus could not have sinned in a moral sense. Their arguments go something like this:

1) Jesus is unchanging. Therefore, if He could have sinned while He was on earth, He could still sin today. Additionally, because God is holy, Jesus is holy and always has been and always will be. Holiness and evil are incompatible, so Jesus could not have sinned.

2) Jesus is omnipotent (all-powerful) and thus has no weakness. Sin is a moral weakness, so Jesus the omnipotent God was morally incapable of sin.

3) God is omniscient, having infinite knowledge. This means that Jesus knew the awfulness of sin and that the plan from eternity past was for Him to be the holy Savior.

4) Jesus the Son only wanted what God the Father wanted, and God the Father wanted Him to be the sinless sacrifice.

In the end, maybe it doesn't matter whether or not Jesus could have sinned. We know for certain that He did not sin, and this is what really matters. Perhaps we can address the question with an analogy: there is a difference between a bird's-eye-view and walking along a road. Looking from heaven, it was clear that Jesus could never sin.

But Jesus, walking the earthly road of temptation, had to fight temptation with all His strength, as if He could have succumbed. And this is why He is our great High Priest. He walked in our shoes yet did not sin, and now He gives us the power to withstand sin as well.

For we do not have a high priest who is unable to sympathize with our weaknesses, but one who in every respect has been tempted as we are, yet without sin.

HEBREWS 4:15

15

Did Jesus know the future?

What did Jesus know, and when did He know it? When people ask this question they are partly wondering what it was like for Jesus to be fully God and fully human. What kinds of limits did His humanity place on His divine foreknowledge? What level of omniscience was entailed in being fully human as well as fully God?

One way of exploring this question is to ask more specific questions like: When Jesus was four, could He do calculus? Could He list the kings and queens of England? Did He know how to rebuild the engine of a 1963 Corvette? Presumably not.

We know that he was born as a baby and grew in wisdom as well as stature (Lk. 2:52). We also know that He was both teaching and learning from the teachers in the Temple when He was a youth (Lk. 2:46-47). It is reasonable to assume, therefore, that in order for Jesus to be fully human He also had to have some mode of ignorance. One of the implications of the incarnation is that Jesus had limited knowledge. There were things that the boy Jesus needed to learn, just like anyone else.

But clearly Jesus did have supernatural knowledge. He knew what was going on in people's hearts in a way that a mere human could not (Mt. 12:25; Jn. 1:48). He knew that Judas would betray Him. He could prophecy about the events surrounding His death and the future suffering of His disciples (Mk. 2:20). His anguish in the Garden of Gethsemane was partly due to the fact that He knew what extreme suffering would come the next day. He also knew that the thief on the cross would be with Him in paradise (Lk. 23:43).

So we can conclude that Jesus knew what He needed to know. Put another way, He knew what God the Father chose to reveal to Him through the Holy Spirit. God the Son chose to take on human flesh, and in doing so He chose to limit Himself to human finitude and submit Himself to the wisdom of the Father in revealing some things but not others.

In surrendering His mind to His Father, Jesus is an example to us. We, too, need to submit to God's will. We, too, are called to walk in obedience to what we know and not strive always to uncover what God is choosing to keep veiled.

Like Jesus Christ, we are able to choose right even though we don't know everything we wish that we did know about the future. And we, like Christ, are to empty ourselves in the service of others.

Have this mind among yourselves, which is yours in Christ Jesus, who, though he was in the form of God, did not count equality with God a thing to be grasped, but emptied himself, by taking the form of a servant, being born in the likeness of men.

PHILIPPIANS 2:5-7

16

What does it mean that Jesus is the Son of God?

The one true God exists in Three Persons – Father, Son, and Holy Spirit. How these members of the Trinity relate to one another is a mystery, but we see aspects of the relationship between the Father and the Son in Jesus' incarnation, when He took on human flesh. It makes sense for us to compare their relationship to the human father/son relationships we experience, and in some ways this gives us greater understanding of the relationship between God the Father and God the Son. In other ways, though, it falls short.

Jesus was not the only begotten Son of the Father in the way human fathers pass on their genetic material to "create" a child. Jesus has always existed, from eternity past, just as God the Father has always existed from eternity past (Col. 1:13-16; Heb. 1:2; 13:8). Neither is Jesus a Son in the sense of being less than God or subordinate to Him. God the Father and God the Son are both fully God, sharing all the glory and attributes of God equally (Jn. 5:18; 14:1, 9; 10:30).

God the Father and God the Son share the intimacy we often see in human father/son relationships. Jesus called God "Abba," the Aramaic word for Daddy. God is only called Father 15 times in the Old Testament, but in the New Testament this title is used 245 times – first by Jesus. For His part, the Father calls Jesus His beloved Son (Col. 1:13; Mt. 3:16-17).

The Father loved the Son before the foundation of the world (Jn. 17:24). The relationship between God the Father and Jesus the Son is one of unique love – a Father's love for His only Son.

> *For God so loved the world, that he gave his only Son, that whoever believes in him should not perish but have eternal life.*
>
> JOHN 3:16

Also similar to earthly father/son relationships, there is a distinction in role between God the Father and God the Son. Jesus was equal to the Father, but subordinated Himself to take the role of an obedient servant. As a human being, He was dependent on the Father to reveal what He needed to know (Jn. 8:28). He willingly obeyed the Father's will and became "obedient to the point of death, even death on a cross" (Phil. 2:8; cf. Jn. 10:18; 14:28). The Son submitted to the Father not because He was less important, but because that was His mission and role.

Jesus' identity as the Son of God is the most important aspect of His identity. It was as a beloved Son that He was sent to earth, emptied Himself on our behalf, died in our place, and was resurrected to glory.

The story of salvation shows us both the love of a Father willing to give up His Son to save His enemies, and the love of a Son willing to submit Himself to His Father's plan even when it meant suffering and dying on behalf of wretched sinners so that we could become children of God too.

17

What does it mean that Jesus is the Son of Man?

We can find many titles or names for Jesus in the pages of Scripture, but His favorite way of referring to Himself was with the title Son of Man. This name is used 82 times in the Gospels, and all of them were from the lips of Jesus. We might think that this title expresses Jesus' humanity, while the title Son of God expresses His deity. But in fact it is nearly the opposite.

To get at the meaning of the name Son of Man we have to go back to the Old Testament book of Daniel, where the prophet says, "behold, with the clouds of heaven there came one like a son of man, and he came to the Ancient of Days and was presented before him. And to him was given dominion and glory and a kingdom, that all peoples, nations, and languages should serve him; his dominion is an everlasting dominion, which shall not pass away, and his kingdom one that shall not be destroyed" (Dan. 7:13-14). This picture shows the Son of Man as an exalted being, appearing in the

Last Days in great authority and power to rule over all things forever. This would have been what Jesus and those who were attuned to Scripture thought of when they heard "Son of Man": not a mere human being, but a ruler with God-like glory.

Those who weren't familiar with Scripture or who didn't have ears to hear spiritual truth would think of "Son of Man" as a general expression meaning "human being." So when Jesus referred to Himself in this way it was a subtle revelation of His identity as the Son of God that would be understood by some and missed by others. Similarly, Jesus told people to keep quiet about His miracles and spoke in parables. He was bringing a spiritual Kingdom, and He didn't want people to try to make Him into an earthly king because that was not His mission. So prior to His death and resurrection, He concealed as well as revealed His full identity.

It is good to consider whether we have ears and hearts that are ready to let Jesus speak for Himself. Do we study all of Scripture so that we can get the full picture of who Jesus is?

Then will appear in heaven the sign of the Son of Man, and then all the tribes of the earth will mourn, and they will see the Son of Man coming on the clouds of heaven with power and great glory.

MATTHEW 24:30

Or do we pick and choose what we want to hear and thus miss some of what Jesus wants us to see? Do we try to force Jesus into our idea of what a Messiah should be and ask Him to take up our causes, like the Jews of Jesus' day who wanted Him to be an earthly king? Or do we worship Him as the divine Son of Man and surrender to His will and purposes?

What does it mean that Jesus was the Son of David?

Jesus' identity was rooted in the Old Testament promise of a Messiah. The royal arc of salvation history begins with King David. God promised David, "Your house and your kingdom shall be made sure forever before me. Your throne shall be established forever" (2 Sam. 7:16).

This promise was reaffirmed later, for example in Ezekiel 34:23 ("And I will set up over them one shepherd, my servant David, and he shall feed them: he shall feed them and be their shepherd") and also in Isaiah 9:7 ("Of the increase of his government and of peace there will be no end, on the throne of David and over his kingdom, to establish it and to uphold it with justice and with righteousness from this time forth and forevermore"). From these covenant promises the people of Israel knew that a forever king was coming from David's family line.

We know that the eternal King is Jesus. Jesus is called "Son of David" seventeen times in the Gospels. This title refers not only to the genetic family tree that ties Him to David (Mt. 1; Lk. 3), but also to the truth that He is the promised King. Son of David is a Messianic title, a formal declaration that Jesus is the long-awaited deliverer who fulfilled all the Old Testament prophecies concerning His royal person and kingly work. That is why when the Pharisees heard Jesus being called by this title they became enraged, charging Him with blasphemy (claiming to be the Messiah) and plotting to kill Him (Mt. 21:15; Lk. 19:47). So the title Son of David reminds us of who Jesus is – the promised Messiah – and what He came to do to deliver us from the kingdom of darkness.

It is instructive to note when Jesus was called Son of David, and by whom. Nearly every time this title is spoken, it is followed by the words "have mercy on me!" "Son of David" is a cry shouted by desperate people who are deeply aware of their need for healing. They

As he drew near to Jericho, a blind man was sitting by the roadside begging … And he cried out, "Jesus, Son of David, have mercy on me!" And those who were in front rebuked him, telling him to be silent. But he cried out all the more, "Son of David, have mercy on me!"

LUKE 18:35, 38-39

are blind, demon-possessed, beggars. At their moment of need, these people cry out to the promised Messiah whom they know can heal and deliver them.

"Son of David" is a cry of faith, grounded in God's covenant promise and the regal majesty of Jesus Christ. It is also a cry for us to utter in our moments of desperation. When we are most in need of God's healing touch, we, too, can cry out, "Son of David, have mercy on me!" And the eternal King who knows and loves us will keep His promise to help us when we cry out in faith.

19

What does it mean that Jesus was the last Adam?

The Genesis account of creation tells us that Adam was created by God in the image of God (Gen. 1:27). He was created sinless and lived in communion with God until He gave in to Satan's temptation and disobeyed God. At that point – the tragic event that theologians call the Fall – every person inherited a sinful nature from birth.

We are naughty by nature and then continue to sin by choice. Because the sinful nature that we inherited from Adam brings death (Rom. 3:23; James 1:15), we can truly say that through Adam, all died. His sin caused all who came after him to sin and subjected all of creation to futility and death. This is what Paul was referring to when he wrote, "For as by a man came death … as in Adam all die" (1 Cor. 15:21-22).

Yet the second part of these verses is where our hope lies: "for as by a man came death, by a man has come also the resurrection of the dead. For as in Adam all die, so also in Christ shall all be made alive." Jesus is called the "last Adam" because like Adam, He was a representative of the people. Both Adam and Jesus were sinless and then made a choice that affected all of humanity. Adam prefigured Jesus and is a symbol or "type" of Him, but as with so many other Biblical symbols, Adam also points out the vast gulf that exists between created man and the eternal Son of God.

Whereas Adam was *made in* the image of God, Jesus *is* the image of God (Col. 1:15). Adam was merely a man, but Jesus was both God and man. When tested, Adam chose sin and brought death to all humanity. Jesus was tested, too, but He chose full obedience to the Father and brought life to all. Adam's sin banished us from paradise; Jesus' perfect life and sacrificial death made it possible for us to regain paradise. Adam died and his body returned to dust. Jesus died but then was resurrected in a glorious body and returned to His eternal throne.

Jesus, the last Adam, has freed us from the curse and consequences of sin. Having become a real human being, He lived a sinless life and died as a representative of the people He came to save.

For if, because of one man's trespass, death reigned through that one man, much more will those who receive the abundance of grace and the free gift of righteousness reign in life through the one man Jesus Christ.

Romans 5:17

He overcame where the first Adam failed, and in so doing He freed us from the curse so that creation is no longer subject to death and futility. Jesus conquered death and brought us eternal, abundant life. How fortunate we are that the last Adam sacrificed Himself to undo all the destruction caused by the first Adam's disobedience!

20

What does it mean that Jesus is the cornerstone?

The cornerstone of a building is placed at the intersecting angle where two walls of a building come together. In ancient buildings made of cut, squared stone, the cornerstone aligned the entire building and thus tied it together. It was the most important piece to get right during construction, because if the cornerstone was not cut square or was placed incorrectly, the entire building would not be structurally sound.

In his sermon before the Sanhedrin, Peter quoted Psalm 118:22 with these words: "This Jesus is the stone that was rejected by you, the builders, which has become the cornerstone. And there is salvation in no one else, for there is no other name under heaven given among men by which we must be saved" (Acts 4:11-12). The apostle drew on Old Testament Messianic prophecy to show how Jesus' message can and must be received. Some people reject Him, but for those who put their faith in Him, He is the very foundation of salvation.

Jesus quoted Psalm 118:22 to describe His coming. This was just after He told the parable of a vineyard owner's son being rejected and killed. In this parable God was the owner of the vineyard, members of the religious establishment were the evil tenant farmers, and the son who was slain was Jesus the Son of God. In telling this parable, Jesus was showing that those who had studied the Scriptures and should have recognized the Messiah when they saw Him, instead would reject and kill Him (Mt. 21:33-46; Mk. 12:12; Lk. 20:9-19). The very people Jesus came to save would put Him to death.

This is a warning for us, too. Knowing a lot of Scripture or being steeped in the teachings of the church doesn't guarantee our salvation or ensure that we will recognize Jesus for who He really is. We want our religiosity to count for something, so it's hard for us to accept that Jesus saves us apart from works or that He cares more about our heart obedience than our church attendance. We can easily become so self-righteous that we don't want to follow Christ when His demands don't fit our preconceived notions of what a Christian should look like. Sometimes we want to avoid feeling guilty, so we reject the idea that we are sinners in need of grace – a truth we need to accept in order to see our need for Jesus.

Jesus' death on behalf of sinners and resurrection to glory is the truth on which the rest of our faith rests. Apart from Him there is no salvation. Building on any other foundation is like trying to construct a building without a cornerstone – it won't survive the earthquakes of life.

The only wise course of action is to build on the foundation of Christ.

> *As you come to him, a living stone rejected by men but in the sight of God chosen and precious, you yourselves like living stones are being built up as a spiritual house, to be a holy priesthood, to offer spiritual sacrifices acceptable to God through Jesus Christ.*
>
> 1 PETER 2:4-5

21

Why is Jesus called the Lamb of God?

From the beginning of history, God made it possible for humans to atone for their sin by the shedding of blood – specifically, by offering an animal sacrifice. Leviticus 17:11 summarizes this concept: "For the life of the flesh is in the blood, and I have given it for you on the altar to make atonement for your souls, for it is the blood that makes atonement by the life."

In the Jewish sacrificial system, a lamb stood in the place of humans, serving as a substitute to bear the punishment for sin. Each morning and evening a lamb was sacrificed for the people's sins (Ex. 29:38-42). Lambs were also slaughtered at Passover (Ex. 12) and on the Day of Atonement (Lev. 16). These sacrifices were a constant reminder that the people had transgressed the law – that they were unable to keep God's commandments and thus were in need of redemption – and that sin brings death. The only way to atone for sin is through death.

When John the Baptist saw Jesus, he recognized that He was the Son of God and cried out, "Behold the Lamb of God who takes away the sin of the world!" (Jn. 1:29). John's audience may have thought back to Abraham telling Isaac, "God will provide for himself the lamb for a burnt offering" (Gen. 22:7-8). They would have remembered the Passover they celebrated each year, commemorating the day when the angel of death spared the firstborn son in each house that had smeared the blood of a sacrificial lamb on its doorposts.

Perhaps they would also have remembered Isaiah's words: "All we like sheep have gone astray" (Isa. 53:6-7). But most of all they would have thought of the promised Suffering Servant described in Isaiah 53, who would be led as a lamb to the slaughter and bear the sins of many. Believers looking for the Messiah expected a final sacrifice for sin. When John called Jesus the Lamb of God, he was prophesying that Jesus would sacrifice Himself to take away sin. This was Jesus' mission, the central event of the gospel: He came to be the sinbearer for His people. His death is our salvation. God Himself became our sacrificial lamb.

For the Lamb in the midst of the throne will be their shepherd, and he will guide them to springs of living water, and God will wipe away every tear from their eyes.

REVELATION 7:17

The book of Revelation portrays Jesus the Lamb of God in resurrection glory: "I saw a Lamb standing, as though it had been slain … and the twenty-four elders fell down before the Lamb … And they sang a new song, saying, 'Worthy are you to take the scroll and to open its seals, for you were slain, and by your blood you ransomed people for God from every tribe and language and people and nation, and you have made them a kingdom and priests to our God and they shall reign on the earth'" (Rev. 5:6, 8-10).

Jesus the Lamb of God was slain to ransom us from the power of sin and to make us His people. Now He reigns in glory, waiting to welcome us into God's presence forever.

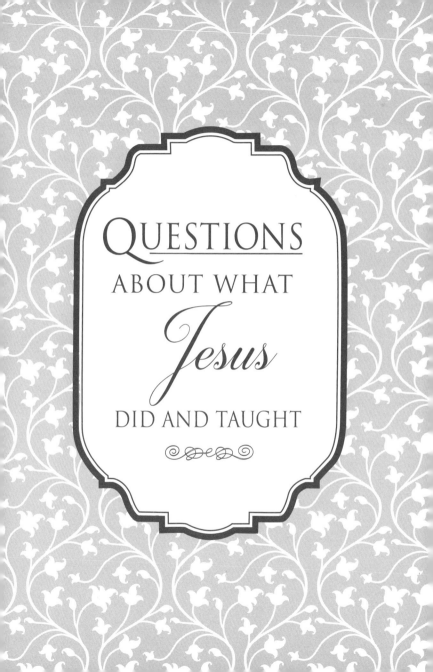

QUESTIONS

ABOUT WHAT

Jesus

DID AND TAUGHT

22

Why did Jesus come when He did, rather than at a different time in history?

Under ancient law, a father had the right to determine when his son would receive his inheritance. In the same way, God the Father fixed the moment in time when Christ His Son would come to earth to give His children their inheritance. Paul writes, "But when the fullness of time had come, God sent forth his Son" (Gal. 4:4).

It was not coincidence or happenstance that Jesus entered into human history when He did. God in His providence had chosen exactly the right time. And Jesus Himself understood the significance of the time: "Now after John was arrested, Jesus came into Galilee, proclaiming the gospel of God, and saying, 'The time is fulfilled, and the kingdom of God is at hand; repent and believe in the gospel'" (Mk. 1:14-15).

While we can't read God's mind and know all of the reasons why it was the right time for Jesus to come, we may be able to discern some of them. To begin with, the Greeks had introduced a common trade language and a culture through which the gospel could be shared across the Mediterranean world.

The Greeks generally believed in an immortal

soul, so that part of Christianity made sense to them. Mystical religions of the time practiced worship that involved bloody sacrifices to appease their savior-gods, so they had a context for understanding the sacrifice of Christ.

The Romans had built a network of roads and an infrastructure to enable safe transport for spreading the gospel. Less positively, Roman oppression caused the Jews to look eagerly and expectantly for the Messiah. The Romans had also introduced crucifixion as a means of execution, so circumstances were right for Jesus to be sacrificed according to Old Testament prophecy. In short, the political and social structures were just right for every Old Testament prophecy concerning the Messiah to be fulfilled in Jesus and for people to be ready to hear and understand why He had come.

From a human perspective, the timing of Jesus' coming made sense and we can see various ways that God had been preparing the world to receive salvation. But perhaps the main reason God sent His Son when He did is that people's hearts were ready to be released from their bondage to sin.

The Gentiles had grown weary of serving their pagan gods. The Jews were just as tired of being enslaved by a law that they could not keep. It was time for humankind to be freed from the consequences of the Fall, so Jesus came to free all people who receive Him from slavery to sin and slavery to the law.

Moreover, He came so that we could be adopted as God's children. Paul continues, "God sent forth his Son, born of woman, born under the law, to redeem those who were under the law, so that we might receive adoption as sons" (Gal. 4:4-5).

We were redeemed at just the right time to be adopted into God's family and live with Him as His children forever.

But when the fullness of time had come, God sent forth his Son, born of woman, born under the law, to redeem those who were under the law, so that we might receive adoption as sons.

GALATIANS 4:4-5

23

Did Jesus say
that He was God?

One common objection to Christianity is that Jesus never said He was God. People scour the Gospels and don't find a direct statement from Jesus about His divinity, so they say that His followers must have misunderstood His intent. But Jesus did make His identity clear, and His original hearers understood that He was claiming to be God.

Throughout the Old Testament, God promised a Messiah who would save His people. The Jews eagerly awaited His coming, and they thought that when the Messiah came He would set up a kingdom on earth. They were waiting for their chance to rule over their enemies. If Jesus had said "I am God," in so many words, some of His hearers instantly would have installed Him as an earthly king. But Jesus repeatedly told those whom He healed not to tell anyone His true identity (e.g. Lk. 5:14) because He did not want the kind of fame that would interfere with His mission.

He came to rule in people's hearts and usher in an eternal kingdom, not a mere earthly kingdom. In addition, Jesus' hearers had no concept of the Trinity, so they would have heard the statement "I am God" as "I am Yahweh," which to them was a crime of blasphemy punishable by death. This would have been counterproductive to His purpose, which was to preach the message of salvation and to die at the appointed time to save people from their sins.

Although He didn't outright say, "I am the Messiah," Jesus made His identity clear in many ways. He asserted His authority to interpret and oversee the Old Testament law when He called Himself Lord of the Sabbath (Mk. 2:28). He taught with authority, not calling on witnesses as other Jewish rabbis did, but speaking truth on His own authority (Jn. 7:15). Jesus claimed authority to forgive sin – something everyone recognized as an assertion of divinity (Mk. 2:7). When Jesus used the phrase "my Father" and called God "Abba," it was a revolutionary expression of intimacy. He was claiming to be God's unique Son. In calling Himself "Son of Man," a title that appears more than 80 times in the Gospels, Jesus claimed a divine title taken from the prophetic book of Daniel. Jesus even alludes to Himself as the great "I AM" of Exodus 3:14 (Jn. 8:28) – a revelation of His deity that would have shocked His Jewish audience.

> *He said to them, "But who do you say that I am?" Simon Peter replied, "You are the Christ, the Son of the living God." And Jesus answered him, "Blessed are you, Simon Bar-Jonah! For flesh and blood has not revealed this to you, but my Father who is in heaven."*
>
> MATTHEW 16:15-17

Jesus' message that He was God was explored openly by the people of His day. Throughout the Gospels, we find people marveling at Jesus' deeds and words and wondering, "who is this?" Their testimony proves that Jesus was not a mere teacher – a rabbi or prophet like others they had seen – but a completely different type of man. Those with open hearts recognized that He was the Son of God, and their expressions of awe and worship should encourage us to respond likewise.

24

Why was
Jesus baptized?

John the Baptist came before Jesus and offered a baptism of repentance. As he prepared the way for Jesus, he said, "I baptize you with water for repentance, but he who is coming after me is mightier than I, whose sandals I am not worthy to carry" (Mt. 3:11). So it is very surprising that his cousin Jesus – the sinless Messiah who had nothing to repent of – came to John to be baptized. Why would Jesus need to be baptized? After all, as John himself said, "I need to be baptized by you, and do you come to me?" (Mt. 3:14)?

There are at least four explanations or reasons for the baptism of Jesus Christ. First, it was an opportunity for Him to be recognized by His forerunner at the outset of His public ministry. John's role was to prepare the way for the Messiah (see Isa. 40:3), and in a sense his baptism of Jesus was a passing of the baton. At that moment Jesus was publicly recognized as the Messiah by the one who had been announcing His coming.

Furthermore, being baptized was an act of submission to

God. Jesus said that this must be done to "fulfill all righteousness" (Mt. 3:15) – in other words, to complete the Father's will for Him.

This leads us to a third explanation: the baptism of Jesus was also a revelation of the Trinity, where God the Father spoke, Jesus the Son was present in bodily form, and God the Holy Spirit descended in the form of a dove (Mt. 3:16-17). The presence of all three members of the Trinity publicly established the authority of Jesus' ministry. The triune God was and is unified in affirming Jesus' divinity and mission.

... having been buried with him in baptism, in which you were also raised with him through faith in the powerful working of God, who raised him from the dead.

Colossians 2:12

Symbolically, baptism was for Jesus – as it is for us – a visual and symbolic representation of His death, burial, and resurrection. For Jesus, baptism was a preview of what was to come at the culmination of His ministry. But He also commands us to baptize and to be baptized, saying, "Go therefore and make disciples of all nations, baptizing them in the name of the Father and of the Son and of the Holy Spirit" (Mt. 28:19).

In baptism, we are united to the saving work of Jesus Christ. The sacrament symbolizes our death to sin and new life in Him. It is a public affirmation of our faith in Christ as well as a dramatic reminder of His sacrificial work that saves us.

61

25

Was Jesus ever tempted?

We cannot truly understand that which we have not experienced. Just as those who are physically strong cannot truly understand what it is like to be physically disabled, Jesus could not have fully empathized with our struggles if He had not faced them Himself.

The Gospels of Matthew and Luke both record a time when Jesus was tempted for 40 days in the wilderness. These are not the only temptations Jesus faced – He was human, so He suffered a lifetime of temptation, just as we do – but His wilderness temptations are recorded specifically for our instruction.

Luke introduces the episode with the words, "Jesus, full of the Holy Spirit, returned from the Jordan and was led by the Spirit in the wilderness for forty days, being tempted by the devil" (4:1-2). The first thing to note is that Jesus was led by the Holy Spirit into this time of testing. Trials and temptations are part of God's plan. They reveal where our true loyalties lie – whether we will trust and obey God or not – and they help us grow.

The author of Hebrews says that Jesus "learned obedience through what he suffered" (5:8). His submission to the Father's will was developed and completed by His overcoming of temptation.

The Holy Spirit led Jesus not just *into* the wilderness, but also *in* the wilderness. God helps us and leads us during our times of testing. He does not leave us alone to fight temptation. Jesus withstood temptation in the limitations of His humanity, unaided by supernatural intervention, and triumphed. We, too, can withstand temptation using the same tools He used: God's Word and God's power living inside us through the Holy Spirit.

The specific temptations Jesus faced are instructive as well. He was at a point of extreme hunger because He had not eaten anything for 40 days. At this moment Satan attacked His physical weakness and tempted Him to turn stones into bread. This was a temptation to mistrust God's provision.

For because he himself has suffered when tempted, he is able to help those who are being tempted.
HEBREWS 2:18

The second temptation was to worship Satan in order to gain power over the kingdoms of the world. God's plan would result in Jesus having power and authority over all nations, but Satan tempted Him to gain the crown without the cross. It was a temptation to take a shortcut and achieve God's will in the wrong way and at the wrong time. The third temptation was to put God to the test. Satan quoted God's Word and told Jesus to test whether it was true. Giving in to this temptation would have been a failure to trust God's Word.

Jesus resisted temptation without falling into sin. He continued to live in grateful obedience when He was tempted. And because He overcame, He can help us to overcome as well. Having been tempted, He understands our weakness. And having resisted temptation, He can help us to triumph.

26

What was Jesus' purpose during His time on earth?

People talk a lot about "mission" these days. There are corporate and family mission statements. People say "this is my mission in life." A mission is an overarching goal that influences all the little decisions along the way. If we know what our mission is, we are able to hold up this or that option against it and decide if it fits or if we need to say no.

Jesus clearly knew His mission on earth and fulfilled it perfectly. A look at the Gospels shows that His purpose on earth was twofold: to accomplish and to proclaim the gospel. Luke thus described Jesus as "a man who was a prophet mighty in deed and word before God and all the people" (Lk. 24:19).

From the very beginning, we read that Jesus came to save us from our sins. The angel told Mary, "you shall call his name Jesus, for he will save his people from their sins" (Mt. 1:21). The very name Jesus points to this purpose, for it means "Savior" or "God saves." Jesus' death on the cross was the culmination of human history, the fulfillment of every Old Testament prophecy about the Redeemer who would rescue His people from the curse of sin and death.

Dying in our place so that we can stand innocent before God the Father and experience a relationship with Him – this is why Jesus came. He said it Himself: "the Son of Man came not to be served but to serve, and to give his life as a ransom for many" (Mt. 20:28).

But Jesus also came to proclaim the truth. He said, "Let us go on to the next towns, that I may preach there also, for that is why I came" (Mk. 1:38), and "For this purpose I was born and for this purpose I have come into the world – to bear witness to the truth" (Jn. 18:37). The preaching and teaching that Jesus did during His ministry years were essential to why He came. God was establishing a new covenant through His Son, and Jesus was the mouthpiece to communicate the specifics of that new covenant. Jesus

> *The saying is trustworthy and deserving of full acceptance, that Christ Jesus came into the world to save sinners, of whom I am the foremost.*
>
> 1 TIMOTHY 1:15

proclaimed the salvation that would soon be available through His death and resurrection and demonstrated what complete surrender to God looks like in real life.

Now that the gospel has been accomplished through Jesus' death and resurrection, we have the joyous task of proclaiming His salvation to others. Jesus left us with this mission statement: "Go therefore and make disciples of all nations, baptizing them in the name of the Father and of the Son and of the Holy Spirit, teaching them to observe all that I have commanded you." (Mt. 28:19-20).

Our purpose in life is to tell people what Jesus has done. And as we do this, we have this promise to depend on: "And behold, I am with you always, to the end of the age" (Mt. 28:20).

27

Which religion did Jesus follow?

Jesus was a Jewish man and devoutly followed the religious practices of His day. His genealogy shows that He was descended from David, and thus was the fulfillment of Jewish prophecy through His royal pedigree. He was circumcised according to the law (Lk. 2:21).

Jesus not only went to local synagogues, but also taught in them and performed miracles there (Mk. 3; Lk. 13). He knew the Jewish Scriptures by heart and quoted them often (Lk. 4; Mt. 5). His family faithfully participated in religious festivals in Jerusalem, such as Passover (Lk. 2:41).

Jesus followed the Jewish law perfectly and completely. He said, "Do not think that I have come to abolish the Law or the Prophets; I have not come to abolish them but to fulfill them" (Mt. 5:17). Jesus defined true religion and practiced perfect adherence to God's law. But the religious establishment of His day had missed the primary purpose of the Old Testament law, so His obedience didn't look like typical law-keeping to them.

In Jesus' day the Pharisees added many regulations to the Old Testament laws given by God. For example, rather than letting the general command to rest on the Sabbath stand on its own, the Pharisees came up with 39 specific activities which were outlawed on the Sabbath – including spitting, since spitting might create a tiny furrow in the ground, and plowing furrows clearly classified as work. In this way, God's laws were weighed down with more and more Pharisaical regulations. These regulations missed the point of the law by focusing on outward ritualistic adherence to God's commands rather than genuine obedience from a heart devoted to God.

Jesus did away with all of this pretense. He perfectly fulfilled God's command to honor the Sabbath, but did not adhere to the Pharisees' regulations. In fact, He went right ahead and healed and performed other miracles on the Sabbath, and also allowed His disciples to pick grain on the Sabbath to satisfy their hunger. Jesus said, "The Sabbath was made for man, not man for the Sabbath. So the Son of Man is lord even of the Sabbath" (Mk. 2:27-28). Thus, He declared His authority over the law and demonstrated true obedience to God's commands.

Let it be known to you therefore, brothers, that through this man forgiveness of sins is proclaimed to you, and by him everyone who believes is freed from everything from which you could not be freed by the law of Moses.

ACTS 13:38-39

Jesus was more than merely a Jewish man fulfilling the true purpose of the Old Testament law; He was also the Savior totally accomplishing the law of God so that we can be declared right before God. Mere human beings can never perfectly obey God's law; we are sinners by nature and by choice and thus are separated from God and destined for His wrath.

But Jesus obeyed the law perfectly and then bore God's wrath against our sin so we can inherit His righteousness. In following God's laws perfectly Jesus freed us from the law's demands so we can enjoy intimacy with God.

28

Why did Jesus teach in parables?

Is there any more engaging invitation than the words "tell me a story"? Stories engage our heart and mind, draw us in, entertain us, and make us pay close attention to what is being communicated. They tell us not just what happened, but also what happens – disclosing truth about the world in a memorable format.

Stories – or more specifically parables – were Jesus' favorite method of teaching. The gospels record thirty-nine parables of Jesus. These parables are long analogies or metaphors told in story form in order to communicate spiritual truth. Aside from the way stories would have engaged His audience, there are two main reasons Jesus chose to teach in parables: to disclose and to conceal.

Jesus told parables to reveal spiritual truth to those who sought it. Apart from personal experience, stories are the quickest way to learn something. We may assent to the truth that God loves us like a father, but when we hear the story of the Prodigal Son we experience God's fatherly affection; we identify with the son's sin and then feel the Father's embrace when we turn to Him (Lk. 15:11-32).

Similarly, we can know in our heads that God takes care of us, but hearing about all the ways He sacrifices for us like a good shepherd brings that knowledge down to our hearts (Jn. 10:11-18). The disclosing or revealing purpose of parables is demonstrated by the fact that Jesus pulled His disciples aside to explain His parables. He wanted to be sure that they (and future readers of the Gospels) fully understood the message He was conveying.

[Jesus] said to them, "To you has been given the secret of the kingdom of God, but for those outside everything is in parables, so that 'they may indeed see but not perceive, and may indeed hear but not understand, lest they should turn and be forgiven.'"

MARK 4:11-12

Jesus told the disciples, "To you it has been given to know the secrets of the kingdom of heaven" (Mt. 13:11).

At the same time, the parables Jesus told were inexplicable to some members of His audience, and this was intentional. Jesus said, "This is why I speak to them in parables, because seeing they do not see, and hearing they do not hear, nor do they understand" (Mt. 13:13).

Those who had closed off their hearts to God were kept in darkness, so that when they heard the parables, they did not understand the message. Knowledge only moves from our heads to our hearts when we put it into action, and those in Jesus' audience who were unwilling to do that continued to wander in the darkness. The same story that seemed like a work of art to some listeners served as a stumbling block to others.

Today we have the advantage of having not only the parables recorded in Scripture, but also Jesus' own interpretation of them in the words He spoke privately to the disciples.

So for us there is no excuse for being hearers who do not hear. All we have to do in order to truly and deeply understand the words of Jesus is read them with a hunger for truth and an intention to obey.

29

Why did Jesus perform miracles?

Throughout His ministry Jesus performed many miracles – events or phenomena that violate or supersede natural laws for the purpose of revealing God to those who have faith. Miracles were also done in the Old Testament, but no one did as many or as spectacular miracles as Jesus did. What was the purpose of all these "signs," as John called them (Jn. 2:11; 2:23)?

The immediate reason Jesus performed miracles was because He cared about people's suffering. Matthew 14:14 says, "When he went ashore he saw a great crowd, and he had compassion on them and healed their sick." Jesus loved people, and He acted to relieve their pain.

A more important reason Jesus performed miracles was to reveal His identity. Isaiah prophesied that the Messiah's ministry would be one of healing: "Then the eyes of the blind shall be opened, and the ears of the deaf unstopped; then shall the lame man leap like a deer, and the tongue of the mute sing for joy " (35:5-6). The miracles Jesus performed demonstrated His authority over nature, thus revealing Him as Creator God. When Jesus performed miracles, He was proclaiming His identity as the Messiah and offering tangible evidence that He is the divine Son of God. The disciples picked up on this after Jesus miraculously calmed the storm. They asked, "What sort of man is this, that even winds and sea obey him?" (Mt. 8:27). The answer, of course, is that He wasn't merely a man; He was also God. And the disciples were beginning to understand this.

The miracles of Jesus drew a huge audience, which Jesus capitalized on to preach His message. Jesus' true mission wasn't to perform miracles, but to proclaim salvation. The miracles were a means to this end, not an end in themselves. They were signs pointing to the coming kingdom of God. There is a lesson for us in this: Jesus never wants the focus to be on the miracle, but on Himself, the miracle-worker. Whenever a ministry focuses on supposed miracles instead of on Jesus, people are in danger of missing the gospel.

> *"The works that the Father has given me to accomplish, the very works that I am doing, bear witness about me that the Father has sent me."*
>
> JOHN 5:36

Ultimately the miracles of Jesus were intended to draw the original audience, and us, into true faith. Jesus told Philip, "Believe me that I am in the Father and the Father is in me, or else believe on account of the works themselves" (Jn. 14:11).

Reading about Jesus' miracles in the Gospels and seeing miraculous answers to prayer today – which is not something God promises but is something that He sometimes does – should enable us to trust Him more. We can pray for miracles in moments of desperation because we know that God cares, but He will only perform miracles when the end result will be His glory – the strengthening of our faith so that we worship Him.

30

Why did Jesus tell people not to spread news of His miracles?

When we think of Jesus' ministry, we often think of the crowds that thronged Him, pressing and following Him to the point where He had to hide away in the countryside when He wanted a moment to pray (Lk. 5:16).

Jesus seemed to be glad for the opportunity to preach to these large crowds, even providing food for them when it became too late for them to find food for themselves (Mt. 14:13-21).

Occasionally after a miracle Jesus would urge people not to spread the word about who He was. On one particular occasion Jesus healed a leper and told him, "See that you say nothing to anyone, but go, show yourself to the priest and offer for your cleansing what Moses commanded, for a proof to them" (Mk. 1:43; see also Mt. 8:1-4; Lk. 5:12-16). Jesus uttered similar words after Peter confessed that He was the Christ:

"he strictly charged them to tell no one about him" (Mk. 8:30). Why didn't He want His ministry publicized, especially since it was already so widely known?

One reason for keeping quiet about the miracles of Jesus is that some people were looking for the wrong kind of Messiah, or the right Messiah with the wrong motivation. They were not looking for a Messiah to serve and worship, they were looking for what a Messiah could do for them. Or they didn't have true faith at all, and were only seeing what the miracle worker might do next out of idle curiosity. Jesus preached to those with "ears to hear," not to those who cared only for the miracles but ignored the message the miracles confirmed.

Other people were looking for the right Messiah, but they expected Him to be an earthly king to free them from their earthly oppressors. However, Jesus came to free men from spiritual chains, not political ones. If people seeking a political Messiah had thronged Jesus they might have tried to force Him to seize power, and in the process compromised His mission to come and die for His people. Or perhaps they would have forced a confrontation that would have brought His death sooner than God intended. Jesus had a mission to fulfill, and at times He told people to keep His miracles a secret because it wasn't the right time for His identity to be revealed.

The message for us is twofold. First, we must be careful to seek Jesus alone, not His miracles. Our goal should be to worship and serve our loving Savior, not to see what He can do for us. Second, unlike these people whom Jesus urged to keep quiet, we are called to speak out. Paul writes, "we are ambassadors for Christ, God making his appeal through us" (2 Cor. 5:20).

And he said to them, "Go into all the world and proclaim the gospel to the whole creation."

MARK 16:15

31

What is the meaning of the Transfiguration?

The Transfiguration was an important event in the ministry of Jesus, even though it was only witnessed firsthand by His closest disciples – Peter, James, and John. About a week after He promised that some people would not taste death before seeing the kingdom of God come with power (Mt. 16:28; Mk. 9:1; Lk. 9:27), Jesus took these three men to the top of a mountain. There they saw His unveiled glory; heard the voice of God say, "This is my beloved Son, with whom I am well pleased; listen to him"; and saw Jesus talk with Moses and Elijah.

All three Synoptic Gospels agree that the Transfiguration took place just after Jesus foretold His coming death and resurrection and shortly before those events unfolded. In other words, similar to the way Jesus' baptism – where God spoke nearly the same words of blessing (Mt. 3:17) – prepared Jesus for His public ministry, the Transfiguration prepared Him for the Passion. God pulled back the veil of heaven for a moment and gave Jesus and His three closest disciples a glimpse of the glory that awaited Him after His suffering was accomplished. This supernatural experience firmly rooted them in the knowledge of Jesus' honor and glory, thus preparing them for the testing they would endure at Jesus' trial and crucifixion.

The appearance of Moses and Elijah on the Mount of Transfiguration may not mean much to modern readers, but Jesus' disciples would have attached great meaning to the appearance of these Old Testament saints. Moses represented the Old Testament law; Elijah the prophets. Together these two prophets represented the entire Jewish faith. But they took on a servant role in relation to Jesus. Their deference to Jesus showed that He was greater than both of them. It also showed that He was the fulfillment of their ministries (Mt. 5:17-19; 11:11; Heb. 3:1-6). As these three men spoke together about "his departure, which he was about to accomplish at Jerusalem" (Lk. 9:31), they revealed that Jesus was about to fulfill all the Law and the Prophets, proving that He was the one to whom their prophecies had pointed all along.

And we all, with unveiled face, beholding the glory of the Lord, are being transformed into the same image from one degree of glory to another. For this comes from the Lord who is the Spirit.

2 CORINTHIANS 3:18

The Transfiguration was not only a revelation of the glory that already belonged to Christ, even while He had taken on human flesh, but it was also a preview of His post-resurrection glory. Jesus was "transfigured" before them, becoming something different than what they had seen before (Lk. 9:29).

The Transfiguration prefigures not only Christ's exaltation, but also the glory that we will one day share with Him. Paul says in Philippians 3:20-21, "But our citizenship is in heaven, and from it we await a Savior, the Lord Jesus Christ, who will transform our lowly body to be like his glorious body, by the power that enables him even to subject all things to himself." The wonder of the Transfiguration is an encouragement for us to press on in our journey of faith, looking forward to the day we will share personally and permanently in Christ's glory.

32

Did Jesus ever get sad or angry?

Sometimes we think that our emotions – especially powerful ones – are bad or sinful. But while emotions can certainly lead to sin or be born out of sin, such as selfishness or pride, emotions in and of themselves are not sinful. In fact, Jesus Himself experienced strong emotions.

For example, Jesus was grieved at the unbelief of the crowd (Mk. 3:5) and indignant when the disciples wouldn't let the little children come to Him (Mk. 10:13). He seems to have been angry when He encountered the cheating moneychangers in the Temple and overturned their tables (Mt. 21:12). These are instances of what we might call righteous anger – anger at rebellion and sin that affronts the holiness of God.

Perhaps the most poignant example of Jesus' emotional life came when He encountered death. In John 11:33 we read, "When Jesus saw her weeping, and the Jews who had come with her also weeping, he was deeply moved in his spirit and greatly troubled." The Greek word for "deeply moved in his spirit" means "to shudder in indignation and outrage." Jesus knew that he was going to raise Lazarus from the dead, so He wasn't grieving because he would never see His friend again. Rather, He was deeply troubled because the situation brought home to Him the evil of death and its tragic consequences for the people He loved. In this response, Jesus fully identified with the human condition and showed that He enters into our grief. He deeply feels our pain over sickness and death because they are a sign that things are not as they should be – the natural order is feeling the results of the fall and God's heart breaks for His grieving people.

When Jesus saw her weeping, and the Jews who had come with her also weeping, he was deeply moved in his spirit and greatly troubled.

JOHN 11:33

Another time when we see Jesus deeply troubled is in the Garden of Gethsemane on the eve of His crucifixion. Mark 14:33 says that He "began to be greatly distressed and troubled." Greek scholars tell us that this phrase describes someone in the grip of horror or terrified surprise. It is a description of mental distress and deep grief, which Matthew describes as "unto death" (26:38). This despair culminated at the cross, where Jesus cried out, "my God, my God, why have you forsaken me?" (Mt. 27:46). The deep grief our Savior experienced in His death is more than simply a proof that He suffers *with* us; at the cross He suffered *for* us. Jesus plumbed the depths of human suffering and faced terror that we shall never face – complete exposure to God's wrath.

The reason we will never have to face anything as awful as the cross is because Someone faced it for us. We are never forsaken by God because Jesus was. We never have to feel the awful consequence of our sin because Jesus did. And we are never alone in our grief because Jesus experiences our grief too.

33

Was Jesus a pacifist?

People who claim to be Christians have done some violent things in the name of Jesus – the Crusades being perhaps the most famous example. Similarly, the Old Testament depicts bloody battles and armed conquest as the Israelites conquered the Promised Land. But Jesus Himself was full of peace and love for everyone and commanded His disciples to put away their swords during His arrest (Mt. 26:52). So was Jesus a pacifist? Does He command us to put away our weapons today?

It is important to note at the outset that when the Kingdom of God is fully realized at the return of Christ, there will be no more wars. In that happy day "they shall beat their swords into plowshares, and their spears into pruning hooks; nation shall not lift up sword against nation, neither shall they learn war anymore" (Isa. 2:4). Christ will rule over a peaceful kingdom forever – which is the world as God intended it to be.

For His own part, Jesus did not fight back at His arrest, trial, or execution. Isaiah had prophesied centuries earlier that "He was oppressed, and he was afflicted, yet he opened not his mouth; like a lamb that is led to the slaughter, and like a sheep that before its shearers is silent, so he opened not his mouth" (53:7), and the Gospels portray Jesus as willingly accepting the undeserved violence done against Him. This was part of the suffering He endured for us. In this way, Jesus is an example to us of "turning the other cheek" (Mt. 5:39) and being at peace with everyone (Rom. 12:17-18).

Nevertheless, there are times when people have a right to defend themselves, and when even war may be justified. Jesus Himself will fight a great war at His Second Coming (Rev. 19:11-21). His mission at that time will be to judge in righteousness and wage war against those who oppose Him.

In the meantime, Christians should stand against injustice and oppression, and sometimes this may involve going to war. In some cases war may be the only way to prevent evil, and in such cases even the tragedy of war becomes a righteous instrument for the justice of God. Fighting an oppressor like Adolf Hitler to prevent genocide, or fighting a civil war to bring an end to slavery, are Biblically justifiable.

Whether or not a particular believer should go to war is a matter of individual conscience and circumstance. Some Christians are pacifists, and their views deserve respect. But Christians who are called to fight also deserve our respect. And there is one kind of war we all need to wage: the spiritual war of fighting against sin and the devil.

For though we walk in the flesh, we are not waging war according to the flesh. For the weapons of our warfare are not of the flesh but have divine power to destroy strongholds. We destroy arguments and every lofty opinion raised against the knowledge of God, and take every thought captive to obey Christ.

2 CORINTHIANS 10:3-5

34

If Jesus is God, why did He pray to God?

The most often-quoted words of Jesus are a prayer: "Our Father ..." These words follow an account of Jesus praying: "Now Jesus was praying in a certain place, and when he finished, one of his disciples said to him, 'Lord, teach us to pray, as John taught his disciples'" (Lk. 11:1). Sometimes we wonder how Jesus, who is God, could also pray to God. Was God talking to Himself? And if so, why?

The answer to the first question is no, Jesus wasn't simply talking to Himself. God is a Trinity – Father, Son, and Holy Spirit. So when Jesus prayed, He was communicating and having fellowship with the Father and the Holy Spirit. That is why He addressed His Father, and also why He prayed in troubling times. Jesus' prayers give us a glimpse of how the three Persons of the Trinity work together in harmonious and organic relationship.

The fact that Jesus prayed also shows us His humanity. He was fully human, and thus needed power (Jn. 11:41-42) and wisdom (Mk. 1:35; 6:46) from His Father. His prayers further show His submission to God the Father, because even when He prayed for deliverance from the suffering of the cross, He prayed "not my will, but yours" (Mt. 26:36-44).

Jesus prayed not only for His own benefit, but also for ours. His prayers are an example to us of how and when to pray. The Lord's Prayer gives us a blueprint or outline for prayer: "when you pray, pray in this way."

Similarly, the high priestly prayer in John 17 shows us how to intercede for the needs of others in the same way Jesus intercedes for us. It shows us what kinds of things to pray

"Watch and pray that you may not enter into temptation."
MATTHEW 26:41

for – unity and protection. Luke 5:16 teaches us to withdraw to desolate places and pray when the pressures of ministry are overwhelming or when we need discernment for the next step we need to take.

The prayers in Gethsemane show us how important it is to ask others to pray for us even as we pray for courage in moments of despair and suffering.

If even Jesus the Son of God needed to pray, how much more do we need to pray! In moments of joy, in times of sorrow, in our hour of deepest need, and for the needs of those we love … these are times when we should follow Jesus' example and pray to our Father in heaven.

He is always ready to listen and respond to us the instant we reach out to Him.

35

Who was responsible for Jesus' death?

Who killed Jesus? Of course, no one wants to take responsibility for such an apparently tragic and heinous event. Pontius Pilate even washed his hands to demonstrate his innocence in the matter. The Bible answers the question in several ways, and in the end we discover that it wasn't a tragic event at all, but rather a victorious one.

On the face of it, the religious leaders of Jesus' day were perhaps most responsible for His crucifixion. They plotted to kill Him because the signs and wonders He performed threatened their position and teaching (Mt. 26:3-4; Jn. 11:47-50, 53). The Jewish crowds in Jerusalem shared in the guilt; after all, they were the ones shouting "crucify him!" (Lk. 23:21; Mt. 27:22-25). Nor can we let the Romans off the hook, either.

They were the creators of crucifixion as a method of execution, and they unjustly tried, convicted, and executed the Lord Jesus. Jesus was killed by an unholy alliance of Jews and Gentiles – they were the ones who were immediately responsible.

The prophet Isaiah paints a different picture of who was truly responsible for Jesus' death on the Cross: "it was the will of the LORD to crush him; he has put him to grief (Isa. 53:10). Far from being a human event outside of God's control, the crucifixion was part of God's eternal plan to save us. In fact, Acts 2:23 calls it "the definite plan and foreknowledge of God." Jesus' death on the cross was the only way God could forgive our sin without compromising His holiness and perfect justice. Seen in this way, the cross is not a tragedy, but a gracious act of divine mercy. It is the ultimate act of sacrificial love, which bought for us victory over sin and death.

There is one more answer to the question, "Who is responsible for Jesus' death?", and it is perhaps the most important answer of all: I am. You are. We all are. It was *our sin* that put Him on the cross, and it was His love *for us* that kept Him there. The second verse of the hymn "Ah, Holy Jesus" puts it well: "Who was the guilty? Who brought this upon thee? Alas, my treason, Jesus, hath undone thee! 'Twas I, Lord Jesus, I it was denied thee; I crucified thee."

"Men of Israel, hear these words: Jesus of Nazareth, a man attested to you by God with mighty works and wonders and signs that God did through him in your midst, as you yourselves know – this Jesus, delivered up according to the definite plan and foreknowledge of God, you crucified and killed by the hands of lawless men."

ACTS 2:22-23

This knowledge is not intended to drive us to despair, for as we have already noted the cross of Christ was God's greatest triumph. Therefore, acknowledging our responsibility in Jesus' suffering and death should humble us by reminding us of God's great love for us and move us to love and serve our Savior with grateful hearts.

36

Why did Jesus have to suffer so much?

The night before His arrest, trial, and crucifixion, Jesus was "sorrowful, even to death" (Mk. 14:34). He sweated drops of blood – a sign of extreme stress – as He poured out His heart to the Father. He begged to be spared the anguish that was coming if there was any other way to attain our salvation.

But there was no other way. So Jesus was unjustly tried, mocked, then flogged until His back was shredded. Many victims failed to survive the beating that Jesus endured. Then He was nailed to the cross and died a slow death by asphyxiation. Jesus' death on the cross was excruciating – in fact, our word *excruciating* comes from the word "crucifixion."

Why was all of this suffering necessary? The suffering of Jesus was necessary to satisfy the wrath of God. God's law demands that we love Him wholeheartedly and put Him before all other loves (Dt. 6:5). But sadly, we do love other things more, and by doing so we defame His glory and rebel against Him. Our failure to worship and serve the great and loving Creator is a serious insult (Dt. 27:26), and the proper punishment for such treason is death. A just God demands a payment sufficient for the seriousness of the crime – and so our sin demanded an excruciating death. To demand less would mean that God is not just. Meditating on the suffering Jesus endured at the cross makes us come to terms with the enormity of our sin and the even greater love of God.

There is also a redemptive purpose to Jesus' suffering. It shows that God can turn the worst evil into good. Killing the innocent, blameless Son of God was the worst possible sin, and doing it by using the most brutal methods man can devise is even worse. Yet far from a tragedy, God used this suffering to gain our victory. Isaiah 53:5 says, "But he was pierced for our transgressions; he was crushed for our iniquities; upon him was the chastisement that brought us peace, and with his wounds we are healed." If the worst tragedy in human history became the greatest triumph, how much more can our own suffering be used for our good and God's glory?

"Was it not necessary that the Christ should suffer these things and enter into his glory?" And beginning with Moses and all the Prophets, [Jesus] interpreted to them in all the Scriptures the things concerning himself.

LUKE 24:26-27

This brings us to a third reason Jesus had to endure such great suffering: in some mysterious way, it heals us. "With his wounds we are healed" (Isa. 53:5). Jesus carried the worst death and pain possible to the grave so that creation could be set free from the death and futility that has held the world captive since the Fall (Rom. 8:20-23). Because Jesus endured pain on our behalf, death has been put to death and we know that one day all suffering will end (Rev. 21:4).

We will be healed because Jesus bore all pain. That is why Jesus suffered – to absorb the pain caused by the Fall and defeat it once and for all.

37

Why did Jesus have to die on the cross?

The central event in the Christian faith, and arguably in all of human history, was the crucifixion of Jesus of Nazareth. His sacrificial death on the cross is everything to believers – our very salvation and hope of eternal life hinges upon it. But in modern times people have questioned why Jesus had to suffer so much. Was there another way we could be saved?

The short answer is no. Jesus had to die because God is just, and justice demands the fulfillment of the law. The Bible tells us that every one of us has sinned and fallen short of God's holy and perfect standard (Rom. 3:23). Since the right and proper punishment for sin against an infinitely perfect deity is death (Rom. 6:23), we were all sentenced to die for our sin. Not to punish us would be unjust.

But God is also loving, and His love compelled Him to provide a sacrifice in our place and thus to satisfy the law's demand. So the Son of God came to earth as a baby and lived a sinless life so that He could become the perfect human sacrifice. When the time came, He willingly took our sin upon Himself and absorbed all of God's wrath for our sin at the cross: "In this is love, not that we have loved God but that he loved us and sent his Son to be the propitiation for our sins" (1 Jn. 4:10).

Because of this loving act that satisfied God's justice, we are given the opportunity to have our final account wiped clean and to have our sins forgiven. Those who put their faith in Jesus are declared innocent and given His righteousness. All of this happens because of the cross, and there is no other way – God's justice and love are expressed in perfect harmony at the cross.

A further question is, Why did this sacrifice take place through death on a cross rather than by some other method of execution? Part of the answer is that crucifixion was the chosen Roman method of execution

Christ redeemed us from the curse of the law by becoming a curse for us – for it is written, "Cursed is everyone who is hanged on a tree."

GALATIANS 3:13

for the worst malefactors at that time. It was virtually the most excruciatingly awful death mankind can imagine, so it fit the awful crime of our sin. In addition, according to Old Testament law there was a special curse for anyone hanged from a tree (Dt. 21:23; Acts 5:30).

By dying on a wooden cross, therefore, Jesus fulfilled the curse that our sin deserves. Meditating on the suffering that Jesus endured on our behalf reminds us both of the depth of our sin and the riches of His love toward us.

38

Did Jesus really rise from the dead?

It's not too much of a stretch to say that if Jesus didn't really rise from the dead, Christianity isn't true. The doctrine of the bodily resurrection of Jesus Christ is just that important. Paul put it this way: "if Christ has not been raised, your faith is futile and you are still in your sins" (1 Cor. 15:17). The resurrection is what proves that Jesus' sacrifice was sufficient and death has been conquered.

Fortunately God didn't leave us without sufficient evidence to prove that Jesus really did rise from the dead. The centurion at the scene, Pontius Pilate, and the men who buried Jesus all agreed that He was dead, and so they wrapped His lifeless body and placed it in a garden tomb. Three days later the women, and after that His disciples, went to the well-guarded tomb expecting to find His body. Instead they found an empty tomb guarded by angels (Mt. 27:57-28:10; Mk. 15:42-16:8; Lk. 23:50-24:12; Jn. 20:1-18).

The linen cloths that had been wrapped around Jesus' body lay in their place, completely undisturbed – evidence that His body had emerged from them like a butterfly from its chrysalis.

The rumor spread by the chief priests – namely, that the disciples had stolen His body – persists to this day. But the disciples' initial disbelief as well as their subsequent willingness to give their lives for their profession of Jesus' resurrection prove that this was no fraud. The disciples genuinely believed that Jesus was risen from the dead.

Jesus appeared in bodily form to many people after the resurrection. Paul says He appeared to more than 500 people at once (1 Cor. 15:6), and there are numerous accounts of His appearances to His disciples. None of them later declared these appearances to be a hallucination, perhaps in part because they touched His body (Lk. 24:39; Jn. 20:26-28) and ate with Him (Lk. 24:30; Jn. 21:12-13). Jesus' post-crucifixion appearances spanned a length of 40 days, during which He offered "many proofs" of His resurrection (Acts 1:3).

The most convincing proof of all is the way that Jesus changes lives. His disciples were heartbroken at the crucifixion. They thought this was the end of the road for the teacher they had thought was the Christ. They fled from the soldiers (Mt. 26:56), and later Peter even denied knowing Him (Mt. 26:69-75; Jn. 18:15-18, 25-27). Yet Peter preached to a crowd of more than 3,000 people at Pentecost only a few weeks later: "This Jesus God raised up, and of that we are all witnesses" (Acts 2:32). Eventually he died for the sake of Christ.

Jesus still changes lives. He turns selfish sinners into people who devote their lives to loving and serving others. He takes people who are His enemies and makes them His friends. And each person He transforms is further proof that He is alive.

---

*Christ died for our sins in accordance with the Scriptures, ...
he was buried, ... he was raised on the third day in accordance
with the Scriptures, and ... he appeared to Cephas, then to the
twelve. Then he appeared to more than five hundred brothers at
one time, most of whom are still alive, though some have fallen
asleep. Then he appeared to James, then to all the apostles.*

1 CORINTHIANS 15:3-7

39

Where was Jesus for the three days between His death and resurrection?

More than mere idle curiosity, this question is raised by the text of 1 Peter 3:19: "After being made alive, he went and made proclamation to the imprisoned spirits" (NIV). Similarly, Ephesians 4:8-9 says (quoting Ps. 68:18), "'When he ascended on high he led a host of captives, and he gave gifts to men.' (In saying, 'He ascended,' what does it mean but that he had also descended into the lower regions, the earth?)" The Apostles' Creed raises similar questions when it inserts the phrase "he descended into hell" between the crucifixion and the resurrection. The mystery that keeps theologians busy is trying to figure out what this means. What was Jesus doing after he died and before He rose again?

One possible interpretation of Ephesians 4 is that it simply refers to Jesus' descent to earth at the incarnation. But 1 Peter seems to refer to a deeper descent – his descent into the grave at his death. In this view the "prisoners" are Satan and the demons whom Jesus defeated at the cross. Another possible interpretation is that at the moment He gave up His Spirit, Christ's body was dead but His Spirit descended into hell, where He proclaimed the victory that He had just achieved over Satan.

It is helpful to consider Jesus' descent into hell in the context of the Old Testament, where Sheol (or Hades) is the place where the souls of the dead go. It is described as a land of darkness (Isa. 14:9; 26:14), with gates and bars that no one can escape (Isa 38:10; Job 17:16). No one praises God there (Ps. 6:5; 88:10-11; 115:17). According to Jesus, both the righteous and the wicked go to the place of the dead, but souls who have rejected God are in torment (Lk. 16:23), while those who trust Him experience comfort and rest (Lk. 16:22, 26).

For you will not abandon my soul to Sheol, or let your holy one see corruption.
PSALM 16:10

At the moment of His death on the cross, Jesus descended to this place of death and tore open the gates of Sheol. He proclaimed the victory he had won and rescued the souls of those who had died while waiting for the promise of His coming (Heb. 11:39-40; Ps. 49:15; 86:13). The situation is somewhat changed now that Jesus has risen from the dead. The souls of those who die believing in Christ now, after the Resurrection, go immediately to heaven to be with Him (Phil. 1:23), but those who die without knowing Christ still go to Hades to await the final judgment (Rev. 20:13-15).

Christ's descent into Hades shows what He suffered for us: He endured death and separation from God. But it also shows us that Jesus was different from us. His body did not decay (Ps. 16:10). He was not abandoned to Sheol like the Old Testament saints. He was raised from the dead, His body and soul reunited, and as a result we who believe in Him will also be resurrected one day. For the Christian, death is the entrance into an eternity with God.

40

What does it mean that Jesus is the resurrection and the life?

Jesus' declaration that He is the resurrection and the life came just after His good friend Lazarus had died. When Lazarus became ill, his sisters Mary and Martha – knowing that Jesus could heal him – sent an urgent message for Jesus to come. But Jesus waited a few days, thus allowing Lazarus to die (Jn. 11:15).

When He finally arrived on the scene, Mary and Martha both exclaimed, "Lord, if you had been here, Lazarus would not have died!" To which He replied, "I am the resurrection and the life. Whoever believes in me, though he die, yet shall he live, and everyone who lives and believes in me shall never die" (Jn. 11:25-26). These words probably seemed like small comfort to the sisters who had just buried their beloved brother and possibly their only male relative, thus jeopardizing their financial security. However, as the day unfolded they began to realize how precious these words were.

By declaring that He is the resurrection and the life, Jesus transformed life after death from a future hope to a present reality. Martha knew the Jewish doctrine that there would be a resurrection at the last day. But Jesus told her that the resurrection is now: It is a reality centered on Me, Martha – a living and breathing person who is here with you, not on a lifeless proposition.

The truth that resurrection life begins at the moment of salvation is substantiated throughout Scripture. Those who believe in Jesus have crossed from death to life (Jn. 5:24). We have been made alive in Christ (Eph. 2:1-6), and thus we have new life in the Spirit (Rom. 8). As a result, we also have the same power that raised Jesus from the dead living inside us, available to help us as we face the challenges of daily life. Just as there are no degrees of death – a person is either dead or not dead – so there are no degrees in the life Jesus offers. Those who are in Christ have spiritual life right now, and the eternal life they are given begins right away, in this earthly life.

> *If the Spirit of him who raised Jesus from the dead dwells in you, he who raised Christ Jesus from the dead will also give life to your mortal bodies through his Spirit who dwells in you.*
>
> ROMANS 8:11

Of course, the resurrection power of Jesus also matters for later. Because Jesus is the resurrection and the life, we do not need to fear death. For those who put their faith in Jesus, physical death is merely "sleep" (1 Thess. 4:14; Jn. 11:11) or a "departure" (2 Cor. 5:1-8), not a final destination. Jesus put death to death on the cross (2 Tim. 1:10; 1 Cor. 15:21-27). Furthermore, at the final judgment we will not be punished for our sin, because Jesus bore the punishment for our sins in order to declare us righteous.

When Jesus returns we will see Him, we will be like Him, and we will live with Him forever (Tit. 2:11-14). This glorious future is ours because Jesus is the resurrection and the life. He freely offers this resurrection life to us if only we will trust in Him for salvation.

41

Where is Jesus now?

The Bible tells us that after the Resurrection Jesus appeared to many people, offering convincing proofs of His bodily resurrection. Then one day "he was taken up into a cloud while they were watching, and they could no longer see him. As they strained to see him rising into heaven, two white-robed men suddenly stood among them. 'Men of Galilee,' they said, 'why are you standing here staring into heaven? Jesus has been taken from you into heaven, but someday he will return from heaven in the same way you saw him go!'" (Acts 1:9-11).

The Apostles' Creed summarizes these Biblical events by saying that Jesus "ascended to heaven and is seated at the right hand of God the Father Almighty." Jesus now reigns in heaven as the Eternal King, and one day He will return to fully realize His everlasting kingdom.

Jesus' ascension and imminent return have wide-ranging implications for us and for our world. The ascension proves God's acceptance of the sacrifice Jesus made on our behalf. His work is done and the ransom for our souls has been paid, so now

He reigns in glory at the right hand of the Father (Heb. 10:12). Jesus ascended to heaven not only to share in the Father's glory and receive the praise that He deserves, but also to prepare a place for us. He told the disciples, "In my Father's house are many rooms. If it were not so, would I have told you that I go to prepare a place for you? And if I go and prepare a place for you, I will come again and will take you to myself, that where I am you may be also" (Jn. 14:2-3). Jesus is continuing His work of rescuing lost souls so that many people can enter heaven.

But Jesus' reign as King is not good news for everyone. Jesus promised to return one day, and at that time His role will be that of Judge. Jesus said, "The Father judges no one, but has given all judgment to the Son" (Jn. 5:22). Unrepentant sinners will face judgment when Jesus returns, and those who have not placed their trust in Him for salvation will be cast into hell (Rev. 20:12-15). The same day that will bring great joy for those who believe in Jesus because it will mark their entrance into eternity with God, will mean judgment and condemnation for those who do not believe in Jesus.

> *But when Christ had offered for all time a single sacrifice for sins, he sat down at the right hand of God, waiting from that time until his enemies should be made a footstool for his feet.*
>
> HEBREWS 10:12-13

We live between Christ's first and second comings. Now is the time to be sure that we have trusted Jesus for salvation so we will be among those who will live with Him forever. And we have the opportunity to tell others about the hope we have in Christ so that His return will be a day of triumph and joy for them, too.

42

What is Jesus' role in the end times?

If there is one event that every Christian looks forward to, it is the Second Coming of Jesus Christ. Immediately after Jesus' ascension into heaven, the disciples received personal confirmation that Jesus would return. The angel told His confused disciples, "This Jesus, who was taken up from you into heaven, will come in the same way as you saw him go into heaven" (Acts 1:11).

Herein lies our hope: Jesus will come back to put everything right in the world. Every last promise will be fulfilled, and those who believe in Jesus will live with Him forever in a new heavens and a new earth.

There are at least three roles Jesus will play in the end times. Jesus' first role in the end times is to gather up His people. Think of the most joyous family reunion you can imagine. It will be like that, only better. Paul describes the scene this way: "For the Lord himself will descend from heaven with a cry of command, with the voice of an archangel, and with the sound of the trumpet of God. And the dead in Christ will rise first. Then we who are alive, who are left, will be caught up together with them in the clouds to meet the Lord in the air, and so we will always be with the Lord" (1 Thess. 4:16-17).

Then Jesus will judge. He will separate those who know Him from those who do not (Mt. 25:31-46). Each of us will stand before Him and be judged according to whether or not our names are written in the Book of Life: "For we must all appear before the judgment seat of Christ, so that each one may receive what is due for what he has done in the body, whether good or evil" (2 Cor. 5:10). Those who trust in Jesus will live in the new Jerusalem, where there is no death or mourning or crying or pain (Rev. 21:1-7). Those who do not trust Him will be cast into the lake of fire (Rev. 20:14-15).

Finally, Jesus will rule as

And to him was given dominion and glory and a kingdom, that all peoples, nations, and languages should serve him; his dominion is an everlasting dominion, which shall not pass away, and his kingdom one that shall not be destroyed.

DANIEL 7:14

the just and worthy King. At that time every knee will bow before Him, for then it will be said, "The kingdom of the world has become the kingdom of our Lord and of his Christ, and he shall reign forever and ever" (Rev. 11:15).

The book of Revelation gives us a glorious description of the new heavens and the new earth over which Jesus will reign. It will be a place of pure beauty, complete worship, and eternal joy. All pain and suffering will be over.

Truly it will be a worthy Kingdom for the worthy King of kings and Lord of lords! This is the source of the believer's hope.

QUESTIONS
ABOUT WHAT
DIFFERENCE
Jesus
MAKES TO
ME

43

What does it mean to believe in Jesus?

We live in a time when things formerly accepted as fact or truth are now considered beliefs or opinions. Many people think you can't really know anything for sure – everything is relative. They say, "your truth may not be my truth, and that's okay."

In this intellectual climate it's hard to have the phrase "believe in Jesus" mean much. But when the Bible uses this phrase, it means eternal life. Romans 10:9 says, "If you confess with your mouth that Jesus is Lord and believe in your heart that God raised him from the dead, you will be saved." Believing in Jesus is the very heart of salvation. In fact, believing in Jesus is *all* we have to do to be saved!

Belief in the Biblical sense of the word does not mean mere intellectual assent. It does not mean simply agreeing that Jesus really lived, or even that He was a good teacher. It is not even enough to agree that Jesus died and rose again. True belief involves action. It is moving from a mental acceptance of truth to personal trust in the person and work of Jesus Christ. Consider the example of a bridge. We may look at a bridge and believe that it will hold our weight. We may even encourage other people to walk out on the bridge and see that it holds them up. But if we aren't willing to walk across the bridge ourselves, then we haven't put our faith into action.

Believing in Jesus means two things: 1) intellectual agreement in the truth of the gospel – God is holy, we are hopeless sinners who deserve eternal death, Jesus is God who lived a perfect life on earth and died on the cross to take the punishment for our sin, Jesus rose again and reigns in glory, and we will one day join Him there; and 2) relying on Jesus – and Jesus alone – for our salvation. Belief is heart and mind, relationship and knowledge, understanding and trust.

> *Now faith is the assurance of things hoped for, the conviction of things not seen.*
> HEBREWS 11:1

Those who truly believe in Jesus have said a prayer that goes something like this: "Jesus, I know I am a sinner. I know that my sin has separated me from you because you are holy. I believe that you love me and paid the penalty for my sin by dying on the cross in my place. Because of Your sacrifice, I know I am forgiven and can have a relationship with You. I put all of my trust and confidence in you. I give You control of My life and want to live for You."

44

How can Jesus be the only way to God?

We live in a pluralistic world that values diversity and tolerance. People hold a hodge-podge of convictions. They want a little Christianity and a little Buddhism and a little bit of something else. The logical conclusion of unrestrained pluralism is relativism, in which people see all religious viewpoints as equally valid and true. In this environment, Christianity is criticized most of all because it claims that there is one way to God, through Jesus, and that anyone who does not come to Him in faith is destined for eternal judgment. Christians are called intolerant; even bigoted.

The truth is that God cherishes diversity. In his vision of heaven John saw "a great multitude that no one could number, from every nation, from all tribes and peoples and languages, standing before the throne and before the Lamb, clothed in white robes" (Rev. 7:9). There is nothing ethnocentric about Christianity – all nations, all languages, all stations of society are welcome. There is nothing elitist about it, either. Christianity is not for those who achieve a certain level of holiness, but for those who realize they have no holiness in and of themselves and rely on His grace alone for salvation. Jesus said, "I have not come to call the righteous but sinners to repentance" (Lk. 5:32).

Christianity is tolerant, too. It respectfully allows everyone to hold and defend his or her own beliefs. Jesus modeled compassion and kindness. He did not manipulate or force people to believe; He lovingly invited them to experience true freedom. This does not mean that we agree or compromise our beliefs, but true Christians will always try to winsomely persuade rather than force someone into believing in Jesus. After all, faith is a gift of the Holy Spirit, not something we can force on someone (Eph. 2:8-9).

Jesus said to him, "I am the way, and the truth, and the life. No one comes to the Father except through me."

JOHN 14:6

In the end, Christianity is either true or not true. If God is the holy Creator of all things, and we are rebellious people (Rom. 3:23), dead in our sin (Eph. 2:1) and deserving of death (Rom. 6:23), then we cannot save ourselves. Jesus said He is the only door to heaven, the only way we can be saved from sin and death (Jn. 10:9). So we cannot believe in a little bit of Christianity and a little bit of something else; it's all Jesus or none of Him.

But rather than being narrow, this truth brings freedom. Jesus accepts anyone who comes to Him in faith – His salvation is so inclusive that it is available to everyone. And His way is simple – believe in the Lord Jesus Christ and you will be saved (Acts 16:31; Rom. 10:9-10, 13). Christianity is not Jesus plus a list of laws, or Jesus plus a pilgrimage, or Jesus plus enough good works to balance out our sins. Salvation is Jesus plus nothing. No one is excluded because of who they are or what they have done. Anyone who comes to the Father through faith in Jesus is saved.

103

45

What does it mean that Jesus saves?

Maybe you've seen a banner or bumper sticker that proclaims, "Jesus saves!" But have you ever stopped to wonder what it really means? Whom does Jesus save? And what does He save us from? Is saving people only part of what He does, or is it the central reason why He came to earth? Luke 19:10 tells us, "For the Son of Man came to seek and to save the lost." Accomplishing salvation was Jesus' mission, the main purpose behind His coming to earth.

The Bible declares, and human experience further proves, that every human being is a sinner (Rom. 3:23). Every time we fall short of God's perfect standard of holiness, we are guilty of sin. Every uncharitable thought. Every selfish act. Every little lie. All of it is sin, and the consequence for sin is death (Rom. 6:23). Because God is holy and just, He cannot allow sin to go unpunished. Therefore, we are facing the eternal, just wrath of God. This is what we need to be saved from.

God is also loving and merciful and desires to have a relationship with us, so He provided a way for us to be saved from our sin and its consequences. Jesus lived a perfect human life so that He could serve as the sufficient payment for our sins. Then He willingly died in our place. At the cross mercy and judgment met in perfect harmony. God's justice was satisfied by Jesus' substitutionary death. We do not have to face God's wrath because Jesus has done it for us.

But not everyone will be saved. Although God will save anyone who comes to Him in faith, those who reject His offer of salvation will not be saved. "But to all who did receive him," the Bible says, "who believed in his name, he gave the right to become children of God" (Jn. 1:12). Action is required from us. We must put our faith in Jesus, trusting His sacrifice and nothing else to save us. The free gift of salvation must be unwrapped and taken to heart or it does not belong to us (Eph. 2:8-9). Jesus saves all those, and only those, who will receive His gift of salvation.

> *For God did not send his Son into the world to condemn the world, but in order that the world might be saved through him.*
>
> JOHN 3:17

If you do not know whether you are saved, but want to be, here is the prayer to pray:

> *Holy Father, I confess to you that I am a sinner. I have done what is wrong in thought and word and deed. But I believe that Jesus died in my place to save me from my sins. I accept His salvation by faith, trusting that His death on the cross will save me from the punishment I deserve. Come into my life and save me. I want to live for Jesus. Help me to live by faith and reflect more and more the life of Jesus in me. Amen.*

46

How is Jesus different from Muhammad, Buddha, or other religious leaders?

In some ways Christianity is like other religions. Judaism and Islam believe in a supreme being. Hinduism, Buddhism, and Judaism understand that humanity has a problem that needs to be solved. Judaism and Hinduism have a god who reaches down to solve a problem we have created. But Christianity has something no other religion has: Jesus.

He is the center and focus of our faith, and in His story and message He is utterly unlike any other religious leader.

Only Jesus claims to be the unique, divine Son of God. Scholars call this doctrine Christ's "hypostatic union" – the truth that Jesus is fully God (Jn. 1:1; Rom. 9:5) and fully man (Heb. 2:14, 17; 1 Tim. 2:5). Jesus is not merely God among men, or even God indwelling man, but both God and man in His very nature. He was born of a woman, and therefore fully human, but also born of the Spirit, and therefore God the Holy Son (Lk. 1:35). No other religion has a deity who took on humanity (Phil. 2:6-8) to save humanity (Lk. 19:10).

Jesus' life was also unlike the life of anyone else who has ever lived. He fulfilled hundreds of prophecies made centuries before His birth – something no other religious leader has done. He is the one and only person who ever lived a sinless, perfect life.

Prophets and other religious leaders performed miracles, but none has ever claimed to have done as many miracles as Jesus did. Nor did anyone else ever do anything close to the scale of raising someone from the dead, feeding over 5,000 people, calming a violent storm, or walking on water.

Jesus' death and resurrection are also unique. No other religious leader died on behalf of his enemies. Romans 5:10 says, "while we were enemies we were reconciled to God by the death of his Son." Jesus did not put our good deeds on a scale to see if they outweighed the bad before He died for us. He did not die only for those who try hard to live a good life. Next to His holiness we are all revolting, rebellious sinners, enemies of God, and He knows the full depth of our sin. Yet He died for us. Then He was resurrected (Acts 1:3), the most amazing miracle of all.

To summarize, what sets Jesus apart from every other religious leader is His desire for relationship with us. He sought out relationship with us by coming to earth, being born as a baby, and living among us. He willingly suffered and died in our place so that we could be with Him forever.

And He did all of this for us not because we are in some way worthy or because of something we've done. It is all mercy, all grace. No one but Jesus loves people like that.

There is salvation in no one else, for there is no other name
under heaven given among men by which we must be saved.

Acts 4:12

47

What do I need to believe about Jesus in order to be a Christian?

Jesus distilled the gospel down to the basics when He said, "The time is fulfilled, and the kingdom of God is at hand; repent and believe in the gospel" (Mk. 1:15). Being a Christian (or "Christ-follower") is really quite simple: repent and believe in the gospel. But what do these terms mean?

To *repent* means to turn away from sin with the intention to live differently. It is declaring that we have fallen short of God's perfect standard and rebelled against Him by serving ourselves or other false gods, and that we long to be made right before Him. Repentance is admitting to God that we have done wrong and asking for a fresh start. We cannot be saved from our sins until we first acknowledge that we are sinners. This is true repentance.

Belief involves not only our minds – giving intellectual assent to what the Bible declares about Jesus – but also our wills, making a decision to stake our lives on God's truth. We must believe that

Jesus is both God and man. This dual nature means that He is able to save us. We must also believe that He died on the cross for our sins. Jesus took the punishment we deserved by dying in our place.

Finally, we must believe that Jesus rose again. His resurrection is proof that His sacrifice was completely accepted and that we are truly forgiven. The crucifixion is incomplete without the resurrection, but the two events together are the foundation for salvation.

It's not enough to believe merely that Jesus was a good teacher, or that He was killed in the first century. In order to save us, Jesus must be exactly who He claimed to be: the Son of God who gave His life to save us from death. Paul summarized the gospel this way: "I delivered to you as of first importance what I also received: that Christ died for our sins in accordance with the Scriptures, that he was buried, that he was raised on the third day in accordance with the Scriptures" (1 Cor. 15:3-4). This is the gospel that saves us – the gospel of the cross and the empty tomb.

> *Everyone who calls upon the name of the Lord shall be saved*
>
> ACTS 2:21

When confronted with the claims Jesus made about His divine sonship, saving atonement, and triumphant resurrection, we have to make a choice. We can either choose not to believe Him, or we can choose to repent and believe, turning away from sin and putting our full trust in Him.

The choice not to believe leads to hopelessness, darkness, and death. By contrast, life with Jesus is peace, joy, and abundant life. It isn't complicated to become a Christian – all we must do is repent and believe. When we make this decision, the blessings that result are vast, both in this life and in the life to come.

48

How can Jesus help me today?

Sometimes we think of Jesus either as someone who lived 2,000 years ago and achieved our salvation by dying on the cross (which He was) or as God who lives in heaven waiting for the time when He is set to return to earth (as He will). But Jesus is also helping us right now. Romans 8:34 says, "Christ Jesus is the one who died – more than that, who was raised – who is at the right hand of God, who indeed is interceding for us." Jesus' work on our behalf continues at this very moment.

Jesus intercedes as an advocate, arguing our case before God. He intervenes and reconciles us to God. John writes, "if anyone does sin, we have an advocate with the Father, Jesus Christ the righteous" (1 Jn. 2:1). The salvation that was accomplished at the Cross is continually being applied to us, so that every time we sin we are once again declared "not guilty" because of the work of Christ. He stands in the gap for us so that we can be righteous before God.

The other way Jesus intercedes for us is as a loving friend. What an amazing thought this is: Jesus is thinking of us. He is bringing our needs to the Father's attention. Jesus lived on earth and suffered all the same temptations we do so that He is able to sympathize with our weaknesses. And now this understanding Savior is standing before God and praying on our behalf.

Together with the Father, Jesus sends the Holy Spirit to dwell in us and sanctify us. In fact, part of the reason Jesus returned to the Father was so that He could send the Holy Spirit, thereby empowering us to live for Him. Jesus told His disciples, "I will ask the Father, and he will give you another Helper, to be with you forever, even the Spirit of truth ... he dwells with you and will be in you. I will not leave you as orphans; I will come to you" (Jn. 14:16-18). Thus, the work of the Holy Spirit in our lives – comforting us, teaching us, and empowering us – is also the work of Jesus. Through the Holy Spirit, Christ lives in us and is with us every moment of our lives.

For Christ has entered, not into holy places made with hands, which are copies of the true things, but into heaven itself, now to appear in the presence of God on our behalf.

HEBREWS 9:24

Far from being a distant God, resting on His laurels and detached from our lives, Jesus is alive and active in our world and in our hearts. It's comforting to know that He loves us as much now as when He died for us.

He has not left us alone to flounder on our own in the Christian life, but lives for us, helps us, and prays for us.

49

What does it mean that Jesus is our High Priest?

In Old Testament Levitical law there was one priest who served over all the others, the high priest. He was held to a higher standard of conduct than other priests and performed special duties that other priests were not qualified to perform.

Most notably, he alone entered into the Most Holy Place each year, carrying the blood of atonement and making intercession for himself first of all and then for the people. The high priest was the person who stood between the people and God as the mediator, interceding for the people.

The book of Hebrews outlines the many ways that Jesus is the Great High Priest, the Mediator to whom all previous high priests pointed. Like those high priests, Jesus taught us, offered the sacrifice and intercedes before the Father on our behalf. But His fulfillment of the high priestly role is far superior to that of the Old Testament high priests.

Whereas the Old Testament high priests were held to a high standard of conduct and needed to be without physical defect, Jesus was perfect in every way (Heb. 4:15). He was "holy, innocent, un-stained, separated from sinners, and exalted above the heavens"

(Heb. 7:26). This perfection enabled Jesus to offer Himself as the final, once-for-all perfect sacrifice. He didn't just bring a sacrifice, He became one. As a result, we no longer need to offer a yearly sacrifice for sins; the price has been paid. Hebrews continues, "He has no need, like those high priests, to offer sacrifices daily, first for his own sins and then for those of the people, since he did this once for all when he offered up himself" (7:27). Jesus was the sufficient and therefore final sacrifice.

In contrast to the old sacrificial system, Jesus' ministry is eternal. The former high priests spent as little time in the Most Holy Place as possible, for they knew that if they offered the sacrifice unworthily they would be struck dead. And of course every high priest apart from Jesus eventually died. But Jesus "after making purification for sins, sat down at the right hand of the Majesty on high" (Heb. 1:3). He is the worthy King of the heavenly throne. His sacrificial work was accomplished and the atonement was complete, so Jesus sat down and now reigns in majesty forever.

Since then we have a great high priest who has passed through the heavens, Jesus, the Son of God ... let us then with confidence draw near to the throne of grace, that we may receive mercy and find grace to help in time of need.

HEBREWS 4:14, 16

Like the former high priests Jesus mediates between the people and God, but unlike them He lives with God the Father in majesty and intercedes on our behalf at all times, forever.

Jesus "is able to save to the uttermost those who draw near to God through him, since he always lives to make intercession for them" (Heb. 7:25). Our Great High Priest continually intercedes before the Father on our behalf, applying His once-for-all sacrifice to our sins. He has done what no merely human high priest could ever do: satisfy the law's demands on our behalf so we can be forgiven and righteous before God the Father.

50

What does John 1 mean when it calls Jesus the Word?

John opens his Gospel with these words: "In the beginning was the Word, and the Word was with God, and the Word was God." The Greek term for "Word" is *logos*, and it refers to the total message or mind of God, the communicated or acted out words and principles that personify God.

The wording of this verse hearkens back to Genesis 1:1: "In the beginning, God created the heavens and the earth." The New Testament mirrors the Old Testament by opening with something else to know about "the beginning" – in the beginning was the

Word. If we unpack John 1:1 a bit more, we realize that in these few remarkable words John is saying that Jesus …

- Is eternal – He was in the beginning
- Exists in relationship with God
- Was with God prior to coming to earth
- Is God
- Creates and gives life.

That's a lot of theology packed into one short verse, and much of it hinges on the word *logos*.

Jesus was the Word of God in the sense that He was the revelation of God. Just as a word for us is a way of communicating, so Jesus communicates to us. But rather than being *a* word – one message among many – He is *the* Word. Jesus is the sum total of everything God wants to communicate to us. He is the complete message. If we understand Him, we understand it all.

Jesus is also the Word in the sense that He is the creative force or breath by which God

And the Word became flesh and dwelt among us, and we have seen his glory, glory as of the only Son from the Father, full of grace and truth.

JOHN 1:14

created all things (Ps. 33:6). He did not start out as a baby – Jesus was eternally existent, the agent of creation, who humbled Himself to become a human being at a set moment in human history. *Logos* communicates Jesus' deity.

Logos is also a mediating word. It conveys God's desire to communicate with us. Far from the impersonal force that *logos* represented in Greek thought, in the Bible it is a personal message. God sent His only Son to show His love. Jesus is the testimony that God first revealed through the Law and the Prophets.

He is the personified instrument for the fulfillment of God's will to save His people. He lived among His creatures to reconcile us to God.

51

What did Jesus mean when He said He is the Bread of Life?

When God spoke to Moses from the burning bush, He said, "I AM who I AM" (Ex. 3:14). With these words, God was revealing Himself as self-existent, unchangeable, and eternally present. Jesus called Himself by the same name, revealing His true identity as the Son of God when He said, "Truly, truly, I say to you, before Abraham was, I AM" (Jn. 8:58).

Jesus combined this name of God with seven Old Testament images that further reveal His nature and purpose. The first of these seven names comes just after the miracle of feeding the 5,000, when Jesus tells His disciples, "I am the bread of life; whoever comes to me shall not hunger, and whoever believes in me shall never thirst" (Jn. 6:35). Just before this, Jesus had miraculously provided physical bread to satisfy the crowd's physical hunger; now He draws on the image of bread and declares Himself to be the source of spiritual life as well.

This image finds its origins in manna – the bread that came

down from heaven in the time of Moses to nourish the Israelites each day while they wandered in the wilderness (Ex. 16).

Jesus made the connection between manna and the bread of life explicit when He said, "Your fathers ate the manna in the wilderness, and they died … I am the living bread that came down from heaven. If anyone eats of this bread, he will live forever. And the bread that I will give for the life of the world is my flesh" (Jn. 6:49, 51). In the same way God sent manna as life-saving nourishment to the Israelites, God sent His Son from heaven to earth to bring eternal life.

Jesus is much more than the manna in the wilderness; that was a sign or shadow but Jesus is the reality. Unlike the manna, Jesus does not merely sustain physical life – He imparts eternal life. And the satisfaction He brings is not temporary, but eternal.

Without Him we cannot have spiritual life at all, but with Him we have it forever. More than that, Jesus brings deep satisfaction to our souls. He is what we long for, whether we realize it or not.

> *"I am the living bread that came down from heaven. If anyone eats of this bread, he will live forever. And the bread that I will give for the life of the world is my flesh."*
> JOHN 6:51

There is one more aspect of the image of Jesus as the bread of life, and that is the image of eating. To eat something is to receive it and assimilate it into our very selves. We use this as a metaphor when we say "that's food for thought" or "let me digest that idea." When Jesus spoke of eating the bread of life, He was talking about how understanding and receiving Him into our hearts gives us life. When we receive Jesus as our Savior we are becoming part of Him and receiving His life inside us.

52

What did Jesus mean when He said He can provide living water?

Thirst was something that people living in the Middle East in Jesus' day understood all too well. It was a hot and dry land, and water was precious. So when Jesus appeared in the Temple at the end of the Feast of Booths or Tabernacles and declared, "If anyone thirsts, let him come to me and drink. Whoever believes in me, as the Scripture has said, 'Out of his heart will flow rivers of living water,'" (Jn. 7:37-38). His words had a powerful impact on His audience.

On the final day of the Feast of Booths, worshipers would process joyously into the Temple and march around the altar seven times. Then the priest would stand up and pour water and wine over the altar. People were thanking God for providing in the previous year and asking Him to continue to provide in the next. The entire festival celebrated God's care during the years the Israelites wandered in the wilderness, culminating in a symbolic remembrance of the time when God provided water from the rock (Ex. 17; Num. 20). At this moment, Jesus stood up in the Temple and declared Himself to be the source of living water. He was saying that their spiritual longing could only be satisfied by coming to Him and partaking of the life that a relationship with Him provides. More specifically, the Holy Spirit would indwell them and grant eternal life (Jn. 7:39).

On the last day of the feast, the great day, Jesus stood up and cried out, "If anyone thirsts, let him come to me and drink. Whoever believes in me, as the Scripture has said, 'Out of his heart will flow rivers of living water.'"

JOHN 7:37-38

Jesus used the same image again in John 4, when He was talking with the Samaritan woman at the well. Jesus said to her, "If you knew the gift of God, and who it is that is saying to you, 'Give me a drink,' you would have asked him, and he would have given you living water" (Jn. 4:10). Jesus was offering the woman eternal life. This was a fulfillment of the Messianic promise of Isaiah 58:11: "And the LORD will guide you continually and satisfy your desire in scorched places and make your bones strong; and you shall be like a watered garden, like a spring of water, whose waters do not fail."

In order to be truly satisfied in this life, we must thirst for and receive refreshment from Jesus. We cannot find true satisfaction in material possessions, earthly relationships, or exciting experiences. Have you tried to find purpose and joy in those things and come up empty?

Only the indwelling of the Holy Spirit through the work of Jesus can bring satisfaction in our inmost being. He is what we truly thirst for. When we satisfy ourselves in Him, He gives us peaceful joy that overflows to others so that we become conduits of the life-giving Holy Spirit and share His love, joy, and peace. The Holy Spirit is the living water that satisfies thirsty souls in a dry and weary land.

53

What did Jesus mean when He said that He is the light of the world?

In the Bible, as in most cultures, light symbolizes what is good and delightful, and darkness what is bad and terrifying. God is light (1 Jn. 1:5), and His people live as children of light (Eph. 5:8-13). Satan and sin are totally dark (Jn. 3:19-21; Acts 26:18), and those who rebel against God perform works of darkness (Rom. 13:12). Unless they repent, they will be lost in darkness (Jn. 12:46) and cast into hell, the land of outer darkness (Mt. 8:12; 25:30). All of these images serve to highlight the great hope in Isaiah's prophecy about Christ: "The people who walked in darkness have seen a great light; those who dwelt in a land of deep darkness, on them has light shone" (9:2). Jesus is the light of the whole world, the one who defines and embodies everything that is true and good and perfect.

Jesus made the declaration "I am the light of the world" during the Feast of Booths or Tabernacles. Each night during the festival the priests would light four candelabra in the court of the women, and the light would glow in the heart of Jerusalem. Its radiance reminded worshipers of the pillar of fire by which God led Israel through dark nights in the wilderness, and the cloud of God's glory that led them each day and hovered over the tabernacle wherever they camped (Ex. 13:21-22; 40:34-38).

Though the Israelites of Jesus' day were celebrating God and remembering His presence throughout their history, they failed to notice that God Himself was right there among them. This explains why Jesus cried out, "I am the light of the world!" God's glory was shining among them once again, in the person of Jesus, but they almost missed it. How easy it is for us to miss His light in the midst of our lives, too. The world can seem like a dark place, and we may be confused by the forces of evil. But the light of Jesus is always available to us if we open our eyes to see Him. Just as turning on a light in a dark room dispels the darkness, Jesus dispels the darkness of sin and fear.

Again Jesus spoke to them, saying, "I am the light of the world. Whoever follows me will not walk in darkness, but will have the light of life."

JOHN 8:12

There is a final aspect of Jesus' light to consider: it is for the whole world. Jesus did not come for the Jews only. In fact, He called them to be "a light for the Gentiles" (Isa. 42:6; 49:6). Jesus came to shine His light for everyone. His truth and His grace are for every sinner in every strata of society.

And He does His illuminating work of bringing light to the nations through people like you and me. Jesus said, "Let your light shine before others, so that they may see your good works and give glory to your Father who is in heaven" (Mt. 5:16). Once we have seen the light of Jesus and been filled with His radiance, He will shine through us so that others can see His light as well.

54

What did Jesus mean when He said He is the door?

In the ancient Near East, sheep were led into a sheepfold each night for protection. This was an enclosure surrounded by a wall too high for the sheep to jump over, often with a "roof" of branches that would hinder thieves from climbing over the wall to steal the sheep. An opening allowed the sheep to enter and exit, but at night the shepherd would sleep across the opening, thus becoming a door to keep the sheep in the pen and dangers out.

Jesus used the analogy of a door to illustrate several truths about what He does for His people. The door of the sheepfold is a means of separating the sheep from everyone else. Jesus separates those who have saving faith from those who do not. When we encounter the truth claims of Christ, we are compelled to make a decision: will we enter into the fold of those who believe in Him, or stay on the outside? Those who enter in receive salvation. One day those who choose to stay on the outside will find themselves outside the gates of heaven, unable to enter in. There is only one door – one way of salvation – and that is through Jesus.

The door also provides protection for the sheep. There is danger from robbers – Satan and his minions or false teachers or anyone else who might try to steal you away from Jesus. There is danger from wild animals – the evils of a fallen world.

Getting lost is a danger as well. Jesus the door offers protection from all these dangers. He said, "My sheep hear my voice, and I know them, and they follow me. I give them eternal life, and they will never perish, and no one will snatch them out of my hand. My Father, who has given them to me, is greater than all, and no one is able to snatch them out of the Father's hand" (Jn. 10:27-29). Our security lies in the fact that Jesus holds us in His hand, and He is far stronger than any-one or anything that might snatch us away.

The door does more than keep us in – it also provides passage out of the sheepfold. There is freedom in following Jesus. Sometimes we might need to stay in the protection of the sheepfold or in famil-iar pastures, places where our faith is easily grown. At other times we might benefit from the freedom of entering new ministries or stretching our faith.

Jesus leads us into places of safety and solitude and healing, and also out into the world to serve, all the while keeping us under His watchful care. The life He gives is one of balance and joy and freedom.

Have you made the decision to follow His voice and experience true life? If you have, then what difference will it make in your life today?

So Jesus again said to them, "Truly, truly, I say to you,
I am the door of the sheep. All who came before me
are thieves and robbers, but the sheep did not listen to
them. I am the door. If anyone enters by me, he will
be saved and will go in and out and find pasture."

JOHN 10:7-9

55

What did Jesus mean when He called Himself the Good Shepherd?

Psalm 23 is a beloved psalm that is often used to comfort people who are going through difficult times – the valley of the shadow of death. It describes all the ways that "the Lord is my shepherd," how He lovingly cares for all the needs of His sheep. Jesus drew on this evocative imagery when He declared, "I am the good shepherd. The good shepherd lays down his life for the sheep" (Jn. 10:11). In this analogy we are the helpless sheep whose very lives are dependent on the Good Shepherd.

Jesus is not *a* good shepherd, as if He were one caregiver among many, but *the* Good Shepherd – the owner of the flock. As such He has a vested interest in the good of the flock. This is contrasted with the hired hands (who represent other religious leaders) who are more interested in their own wealth and well-being than that of the flock. In a moment of grave danger they will run away to save themselves rather than giving their lives for the sheep.

We are like senseless, helpless, dirty sheep – yet Jesus the Good Shepherd gave His life for us. This truth is all the more awe-inspiring when we think of the place that sheep had in the sacrificial system of the Old Testament. Under the old covenant many sheep were sacrificed for the sins of shepherds and other Israelites who needed God's grace. Under the new covenant the shepherd dies for the sheep, and His one-time sacrifice atones for the sin of the whole world.

The Good Shepherd knows His sheep, and they know Him (Jn. 10:14). The Greek word for *know* connotes intimacy, understanding, choice, and love. Jesus the Good Shepherd knows the characteristics and weaknesses of each sheep in His flock. He knows our past hurts, the ways we are prone to wander, our idiosyncrasies, and what motivates us. Because He knows everything about us, He knows exactly what we need. And He loves us, so we can trust that He will meet all of our needs and do what is best for us.

As simpleminded as sheep are, they do know enough to recognize their shepherd by his voice and refuse to follow any other shepherd (Jn. 10:3-5). They are able to recognize what a particular tone of voice or movement means and respond appropriately. The more time we spend with Jesus, the more we come to recognize His voice and respond to His leading. And lead us He does – calling us into His will and guiding us in the right paths.

"I am the good shepherd. I know my own and my own know me, just as the Father knows me and I know the Father; and I lay down my life for the sheep."

JOHN 10:14-15

He takes us to green pastures and leads us beside still waters. Sometimes Christians are afraid they will miss God's will for them or inadvertently be led away from the right path. But if we are truly seeking to follow our Good Shepherd, He will show us which way to go and will not allow us to be led astray.

56

What did Jesus mean when He said that He is the true vine?

Jewish heritage was rich with symbols of fruit-bearing vines. For example, they adorned the Temple as a reminder that God had said, "For the vineyard of the LORD of hosts is the house of Israel, and the men of Judah are his pleasant planting" (Isa. 5:7). This image was further expounded in other passages, most notably Ezekiel 15 and 17. God took care of Israel the way a careful gardener tends to a vine, but rather than bearing fruit as they should have, Israel rebelled against Him and was cast into the fire.

Jesus took this Old Testament image of the vine and applied it to Himself, saying He not only cares for the vine, but also gives His very life to the branches. In an extended analogy, He compared Himself to the vine, God the Father to the gardener, and His people to the branches. We draw on Christ's life to bear fruit for His glory. The same lifeblood that flows through Him flows out into us. And when we are fulfilling our purpose, we will bear fruit. Fruit-bearing is the identifying mark of a believer, the unmistakable sign of spiritual health and vital connection to Jesus.

The fruit that believers bear includes leading people to Christ (Rom. 1:13), but it is certainly not limited to that. Jesus is talking about the reproduction of the life of the vine in the branches. Paul outlines the fruitful characteristics of personal holiness that the Spirit produces in us: "love, joy, peace, patience, kindness, goodness, faithfulness, gentleness, self-control" (Gal. 5:22-23).

"I am the vine; you are the branches. Whoever abides in me and I in him, he it is that bears much fruit, for apart from me you can do nothing."

JOHN 15:5

Worship is another fruit that the life of Christ produces in us (Heb. 13:15). So are good works (Mt. 5:13-16; Col. 1:10). Any way in which we become more like Christ and reproduce His life in others is an example of bearing fruit.

Just as a branch cannot bear fruit if it is severed from the vine, so we must remain connected to Jesus in order to have a vibrant and productive spiritual life. Jesus says that we can do nothing without Him. It is not that we are merely hindered in our productiveness without Him; rather, we are truly helpless to produce true fruit on our own. What might look like kingdom service is worthless if God is not in it.

Our union with Jesus depends on His initiation, but the ongoing communion that enables us to bear fruit also depends on our trust and obedience. God the Father creates the environmental conditions that will make us productive, giving us a perfectly healthy plant to grow on, providing sunshine and rain, and pruning the branches that aren't bearing fruit so that the harvest will be greater.

But it is our responsibility to remain in Him – keeping our union with Christ strong by purposefully attending to our relationship with Him through prayer, Bible study, and fellowship with other believers. These are the ways we abide in Jesus and are essential for us to bear healthy spiritual fruit.

57

In what ways do we share in the suffering of Christ?

One of the most disconcerting promises in Scripture, coming straight from the lips of Jesus, is "If they persecuted me, they will also persecute you" (Jn. 15:20). Similarly, Jesus said, "In the world you will have tribulation" (Jn. 16:33). Not only did our Savior promise that we would experience hardship and persecution, but He also went so far as to say that we are blessed when we do: "Blessed are you when others revile you and persecute you and utter all kinds of evil against you falsely on my account. Rejoice and be glad, for your reward is great in heaven" (Mt. 5:11-12).

What are we to make of these troubling promises and difficult blessings? Should we desire suffering and pursue persecution? Of course, it is human nature to avoid pain. We try to stay out of danger and seek medical assistance when we experience physical pain. We pray for deliverance from emotional suffering. We sometimes neglect to share the gospel because we are afraid of rejection or ridicule. In so many ways we protect ourselves against pain. But Jesus says that there is blessing in persecution and suffering.

Suffering of any kind helps us identify with Christ. He suffered for us in achieving our salvation (Isa. 53:5). When we suffer, we understand a bit of what Jesus went through and appreciate more deeply the love Christ showed when He willingly took on the physical and emotional horrors of the Cross on our behalf. Pain helps us experience Christ's love in a new and more personal way.

Paradoxically, our suffering also helps others see Christ's love. Paul writes, "Now I rejoice in my sufferings for your sake, and in my flesh I am filling up what is lacking in Christ's afflictions for the sake of his body, that is, the church" (Col. 1:24). The apostle is not saying that Christ's suffering was in any way insufficient for our salvation.

There is one redeemer, Jesus Christ, and the atonement He offered at the Cross is complete. But when we suffer for the sake of Christ, we fulfill God's strategy for gospel proclamation. Suffering is not only a consequence of sharing the gospel; it is the method by which the gospel goes forth as the perseverance of a persecuted church demonstrates the reality of the Cross. The lives of the martyrs throughout history show over and over again that when believers are persecuted and killed, the gospel flourishes.

"I have said these things to you, that in me you may have peace. In the world you will have tribulation. But take heart; I have overcome the world."

JOHN 16:33

But it's not just bloodshed that spreads the gospel. Anytime Christians make personal sacrifices on behalf of others they are demonstrating the message of the gospel. Paul put it this way: "For we who live are always being given over to death for Jesus' sake, so that the life of Jesus also may be manifested in our mortal flesh" (2 Cor. 4:11). Our suffering for others shows them Jesus' love. It makes His sacrifice visible and personal. Pouring ourselves out for others is not in vain – God uses it for His glory and their salvation.

58

What does it mean that Jesus is the firstfruits of those who have died?

The firstfruits were the first part of any harvest. The first fruit or grain a farmer gathered was to be dedicated to God: "The best of the first-fruits of your ground you shall bring into the house of the LORD your God" (Ex. 23:19).

The feast of firstfruits (Nissan) was held on the third day after Passover to ceremoniously offer the first of the harvest as an offering of worship (Lev. 23:9-14).

The firstfruits were special not only because they were first, but also because they held the promise that the rest of the harvest would occur. Dedicating these to God signified that the people were giving God the best they had to offer and trusting Him to provide the remaining harvest to care for their needs.

The Old Testament tradition of the firstfruits proves the background for what Paul wrote to the

Corinthians: "Christ has been raised from the dead, the firstfruits of those who have fallen asleep" (1 Cor. 15:20).

The apostle was speaking of more than the chronological precedence of Christ's resurrection. He was linking it to the Jewish offering of the firstfruits. Because Jesus was crucified on Passover, the day of His resurrection would have fallen on the day of the feast of the firstfruits. This was yet another example of how Jesus fulfilled all the Old Testament symbols that pointed to Him.

Jesus' resurrection was the firstfruits of the resurrection because it was a completely new kind of event – the beginning of the renewal of all things. Other people had been raised from the dead (including Lazarus not too long before), but they remained mortal and eventually all of them died. Only Jesus received His resurrection body immediately and was raised to eternal life, never to die again. Thus He was the beginning of the harvest of resurrected, imperishable bodies that will be gathered at His return.

So is it with the resurrection of the dead. What is sown is perishable; what is raised is imperishable. It is sown in dishonor; it is raised in glory. It is sown in weakness; it is raised in power. It is sown a natural body; it is raised a spiritual body.

1 CORINTHIANS 15:42-44

Like the firstfruits of a harvest, Jesus' resurrection to eternal life is a guarantee that one day we will be raised to eternal life.

Paul concludes his argument: "For as in Adam all die, so also in Christ shall all be made alive. But each in his own order: Christ the firstfruits, then at his coming those who belong to Christ" (1 Cor. 15:22-23). We can know that one day we will receive new, resurrected, imperishable bodies because Jesus was raised from the dead. God will gather the rest of the harvest of those who belong to Him at the final resurrection. In the meantime, we can celebrate Christ's resurrection as the guarantee of our eternal hope.

59

When will Jesus come again?

Jesus ascended to Heaven with the promise that He would return. It was a hopeful promise that gave His disciples – and gives us – something to live for and look forward to. Jesus is the conquering King who will come to make everything right that has been wrong since the Fall. He will restore all things to the way they were supposed to be – all suffering ended, all sin removed, and creation freed from its bondage to death. The assurance of His glorious appearing is indeed a blessed hope (Tit. 2:13).

In fact, some believers are so excited about the day when Christ will return that they have tried to predict the date and make a timeline of how events will unfold.

We know from Scripture that no one can know the exact time of Christ's return. It will be unexpected. Jesus told His disciples, "But concerning that day and hour no one knows, not even the angels of heaven, nor the Son, but the Father only" (Mt. 24:36). Scripture compares the second coming to labor pains coming on a woman about to give birth (Mt. 24:8) or to a thief breaking into a house (Mt. 24:43).

We will be going about our business, working, "eating and drinking, marrying and giving in marriage," and suddenly He will appear (Mt. 24:37-41). Those who say they have figured out the formula and can predict the day when Christ will return are false prophets. But since we know that it will be unexpected – and soon – we need to be ready for it at any time. We should live each day as if it might be our last, giving our best to the work God has given us and sharing His love with others so they can be saved.

We also know that Christ's return will follow certain signs. Jesus outlined some of these in Matthew 24 and Luke 21, saying that before the end of the world there would be earthquakes, wars, and famines. Paul predicted godlessness and false teaching in 2 Timothy 3-4, and Peter spoke of the heavens passing away with a roar (2 Pet. 3:10). Other end-times prophecies predict that Israel will return to its own land (Ezek. 36:8-12) and Jerusalem will be restored (Lk. 21:24), its neighbors will attack (Ezek. 38:2-6),

He who testifies to these things says, "Surely I am coming soon." Amen. Come, Lord Jesus!

REVELATION 22:20

there will be some type of world power and religion (Rev. 13), and Babylon will reemerge as a world power (Rev. 18:2-3).

None of these predicted signs comes with a precise date, and all of them are mysteries. They also happen to sound rather terrifying, but those who are in Jesus need not fear. For us the return of Jesus Christ will be a homecoming, because "our citizenship is in heaven, and from it we await a Savior, the Lord Jesus Christ" (Phil. 3:20). We will appear with Jesus in glory (Col. 3:4). We will gaze at our Savior and worship Him face to face. So it is no wonder that Christians through the ages have eagerly awaited Christ's return!

60

What does it mean to be a joint heir with Christ?

In the ancient world inheritance played an important role in society. Sons received property upon the death of their fathers, including land and possessions. This is how the family name and property was maintained throughout the generations.

In Jewish culture the oldest son received a double share of the inheritance, but by New Testament times Greek and Roman culture had influenced the practice of inheritance so that all legitimate heirs shared equally and jointly in their father's estate. Inheritance had both an immediate application of providing material goods to the heirs and implications for the future as property passed from generation to generation. Adopted children as well as natural offspring received an inheritance.

Paul takes the practice of an inheritance and applies it symbolically to our spiritual adoption into God's family: "The Spirit himself bears witness with our spirit that we are children of God, and if children, then heirs – heirs of God and fellow heirs with Christ, provided we suffer with him in order that we may also be glorified with him" (Rom. 8:16-17). Our relationship with Jesus entitles us to a full share in His inheritance. People who are redeemed through their faith in Christ become children of God, adopted into His family, which means we share everything that Jesus the Son of God inherits. God the Father holds nothing back from us, but generously lavishes every spiritual gift on us.

And because you are sons, God has sent the Spirit of his Son into our hearts, crying, "Abba! Father!" So you are no longer a slave, but a son, and if a son, then an heir through God.

GALATIANS 4:6-7

When we think of our inheritance in Christ, probably the first thing that comes to mind is heaven. This is the future inheritance which we eagerly await – what Peter calls "an inheritance that is imperishable, undefiled, and unfading, kept in heaven for you" (1 Pet. 1:4). The assurance of an eternal home in heaven gives us hope as we await the consummation of all things at the end of human history.

There is also an immediate aspect to the inheritance we have in Christ. The Holy Spirit is a down payment of the spiritual blessings that await us. Paul wrote to the Ephesians: "In him you also, when you heard the word of truth, the gospel of your salvation, and believed in him, were sealed with the promised Holy Spirit, who is the guarantee of our inheritance until we acquire possession of it, to the praise of his glory" (1:13-14).

The Holy Spirit lives inside us and pours God's power, love, comfort, peace, and joy in our hearts. The Spirit's work in and through us is an immediate blessing that helps us grow into the likeness of Christ; it is also a guarantee that we belong to God and will spend eternity with Him. The presence of the Holy Spirit both empowers and encourages us as we strive to follow Jesus each day.

Nancy Taylor

has spent the past 17 years
raising her brood of five children
while maintaining an active freelance
writing and editing schedule. Born
and raised in Wheaton, Illinois,
she is a graduate of Wheaton College
with a degree in English and
Christian Education.

Philip Ryken

is President of Wheaton College.
A graduate of Wheaton College,
Westminster Theological Seminary,
and the University of Oxford,
Dr. Ryken is the author of more than
forty Bible commentaries and
other books on Christianity and culture.
He also serves as a board member for
the Lausanne Movement and the
National Association of Evangelicals.

Notes